MAKING DOLLS

Ilse Gray

Drawings by David Gray

Photographs by Michael Wickham

Studio Vista London

For Alice and Adam

The author would like to thank Marion Fiddimore for her help
and suggestions in testing some of the patterns

1695· 77

Editor · Brenda Herbert
Designer · Ian Craig
First published in Great Britain by
Studio Vista Publishers, Blue Star House,
Highgate Hill, London N.19
and in the United States by
Watson-Guptill Publications
165 West 46th Street, New York, NY 10036
Library of Congress Catalog Card Number
Set in 10 pt Times new roman 1 pt leaded
Printed in Great Britain by
Richard Clay (The Chaucer Press) Ltd
Bungay, Suffolk

ISBN   0 289 70199 6

Contents

Introduction

Making a doll at home for a particular child is a very different matter from going out and choosing one, however carefully, in a toy shop—quite apart from the difference in cost. For one thing, the child knows that you have spent a lot of time doing something for him or her alone and will treasure it all the more for that reason. For another, creating something unique is an enjoyable experience. There must be many people who have wanted to try their hand at doll-making but have been put off because they lacked the necessary needlework experience to understand the seemingly complicated instructions often found in paper dress patterns.

One aim of this book is to encourage beginners, and I have tried to keep instructions as simple and explicit as I can and to avoid elaborate details which, while they may be important to the proper fitting and comfort of a human garment, are unnecessary in a doll—which doesn't after all move about and won't know the difference. These dolls are all made of fabric and are arranged in order of simplicity; the easiest at the beginning, the more difficult ones towards the end.

The book also aims to provide new ideas for those more experienced at sewing, and the suggestions and illustrations can be used as a starting point rather than copied in exact detail. For this reason also the clothes, while kept simple, are made from as many different patterns as possible, so that they can be adapted. Some people may want to make only a doll's body and to knit or crochet the clothes. Others may be skilled at embroidery.

I have tried to include a good cross-section both of basic dolls—the sort that can be dressed and undressed and put to bed—and character dolls whose clothes are an integral part of their identity. The latter are also more acceptable to boys, as are the glove puppets. Current fashions, which change quickly, have been avoided, and period dresses are intended to give a general impression rather than being true to any specific date.

Soft dolls are not a recent invention. They can be traced right back in history, and examples can be seen in museum collections. They were not always used as toys, but often as religious or fertility symbols. There is a Roman rag doll in the British Museum which was found in a child's grave dating back to 300 B.C. Other early finds include first-century Peruvian dolls made of woven materials and sixth-century Coptic dolls made of brightly coloured wools.

Fabric dolls have always been particularly suited to home craft because few materials and virtually no special equipment is needed. Those made by our great-great-grandmothers were probably similarly constructed to some of the dolls here; and many have also been successfully manufactured commercially. Because they were unbreakable and cheaper they tended to get more wear from their owners, who were made to treat expensive dolls with care and respect—one reason why there are so many more beautiful examples of wax, bisque or composition dolls in elaborate costumes in the museums today than there are rag dolls.

I hope this book will encourage the hesitant and also stimulate those with more experience to create their own ideas by adapting the patterns to suit themselves.

1 Materials, methods and tools

Before starting to make any doll, it is helpful to have a general picture of what materials are available, suitable fabrics for each purpose, the tools you will need and an over-all look at the various stages of cutting and making leading to the finished doll.

Materials

Fabrics

Almost any fabric that comes to hand can be used in doll-making, but some are obviously better than others. Left-over pieces from dressmaking or furnishing, or an out-of-date garment, can be utilized and many people keep a rag bag especially for this purpose. Others find that half the fun consists of going out and selecting and matching exactly the right fabrics you want. It is worth remembering that only a relatively small amount of fabric is required, so the cost need not be high. Never make anything out of fabric you don't like.

Avoid fabrics that fray easily as they are difficult to work with on such a small scale and if used for the body are more likely to come undone at the seams, particularly in the curves. When using old clothes or pieces from the rag bag, make sure the material has not worn thin, as children can give a doll a lot of rough treatment and a tired or worn fabric tears more easily. Thick fabrics are bulky and out of scale, very flimsy fabrics and those that crease easily should be avoided in most cases. The following are some suggestions for suitable fabrics:

Body: Flesh-coloured cotton, cotton poplin, calico, flannelette, winceyette, stockinette, some linen, polyester or other synthetic fibres such as Dacron, or polyester/cotton mixtures. Make sure the fabric is strong enough to withstand the strain of stuffing. Choose a pale pink, rather than a strong harsh one. Unbleached calico also makes a good doll's body; so do old linen sheets. There is usually a choice of browns and beiges in cotton poplin for oriental or African dolls. Felt can also be used, but not on dolls you may want to wash.

Dresses: Most of the above, plus others like silk, rayon, Vyella, Courtelle or other acrylic fibres or mixtures, light wool or wool mixtures. Ginghams and printed cottons are cheap, hard-wearing, wash well and don't fray, and there is a wide choice. Dolls in period costumes look better in traditional patterns such as stripes or checks, and fabrics similar to those of the period. Lightweight velvet can also be used. Where a raw edge has to be left—as on the jester's tunic in chapter 6—felt is practical. The glove puppets in chapter 9 are also made entirely of felt.

Trousers or shorts: Denim or other strong cotton, fine needlecord, medium worsteds, etc.

Underwear: Lightweight cotton, lawn, cambric, nylon or other synthetic fibres, broderie anglaise. Also old cotton sheets, petticoats or even shirts.

N.B. Throughout the book, the amount of yardage given refers to fabric 36 in. wide.

Stuffing

The most readily available material for stuffing dolls is kapok, and for this reason I have suggested it throughout the book. It is soft and light and gives a firm, unlumpy result; and because it is light in colour it won't show through fabric. It can, however, be fairly expensive. There are other equally good—sometimes better—materials used by toy manufacturers and upholsterers. These include rayon fillings, cotton flock, mill puff and various industrial synthetic wastes. Some of these, for instance the synthetic wastes, wash very well (unlike kapok), some are fire-resistant, some of the less good ones tend to get lumpy and heavy, but most of them cannot be bought in retail shops or only through a small number of outlets (see suppliers list at end of book). You may possibly be able to buy some through a kindly upholsterer.

Foam pieces are not really very satisfactory and tend to look lumpy. It is possible to use cut up nylons, but a large number of them are needed and the doll will be heavier—and if the stockings or tights are dark-coloured the stuffing may show through.

Trimmings, accessories, etc.
Some large stores have excellent haberdashery departments, where you can find ribbons, velvets, lace, broderie anglaise, braids, fringing and allied trimmings by the yard in a variety of colours and at a variety of prices. If you are stuck for an idea, walking round a shop of this kind can re-inspire you. Hunting through left-overs from past dressmaking often produces interesting finds, and of course old lace, whether hand- or machine-made, is ideal particularly for a period doll, as the faded quality adds to the authenticity. Other useful accessories include buttons, brass curtain rings, buckles, beads, feathers, sequins and artificial flowers.

Hair
The most suitable hair material for the dolls in this book is knitting wool (yarn): double- or triple-knitting wool, or thinner if you prefer, particularly for the smaller dolls and the miniature ones. Some Courtelle or nylon/wool mixtures have a shine to them which goes well with certain dolls—for instance the smooth black hair of an Indian. Crepe wool is also effective. In chapter 6 I have used dishcloth cotton, which is slightly heavier and denser than wool. Other materials, such as thick embroidery threads or even raffia, have been used successfully in doll-making elsewhere, and this is a matter of choice.

Tools and other sewing aids

Tools needed for doll-making are few and simple and can be found in most homes. The following is a list of useful items, but you will not necessarily need them all:
Sharp scissors
Small pointed scissors (for trimming corners, etc.)
Pinking shears
Assorted needles for sewing, embroidery and wool (yarn)
Long thin upholstery needle (for sewing on limbs)
Pins
Narrow elastic and shirring elastic
Button thread (for sewing on limbs)
Snap fasteners
Machine cotton thread in assorted colours
Embroidery cotton thread in assorted colours
Bias binding in assorted colours
Petersham ribbon
Tape measure
Tailor's chalk

Latex glue (e.g. Copydex, Sobo, Elmer's)
Ruler, set square, compass, pencils
Squared paper (see below) or plain paper
Tracing or detail paper
Cardboard roll, 1 in. diameter (glove puppets)
Pipe cleaners (miniature dolls)
Knitting needle (for stuffing)
Canvas or buckram (for stiffening hats)

Methods

Detailed instructions for making individual dolls are given in each chapter, but there are steps in the making process which are common to all or at least some of them and which it would be tedious to repeat each time. The following section should be read through before starting on the practical work, particularly for those unfamiliar with dressmaking. It can also be referred to later. (Hair and features are dealt with in the next chapter.)

Patterns

All patterns for the dolls and their clothes will be found at the end of the book, drawn on a squared grid. To full size, these squares should measure 1 in.; so to make a full-size pattern you will need a sheet of paper marked out in 1-in. squares. (If a larger or smaller doll is wanted, the squares can be made larger or smaller as required—for instance $1\frac{1}{4}$ in. or $\frac{3}{4}$ in.) With a ruler and set square draw parallel horizontal lines 1 in. apart, then vertical ones at right angles to them. Alternatively, it is possible to buy printed sheets of 1-in. squared paper from stationers' shops, but usually these are subdivided into smaller squares and to avoid mistakes the 1-in. intervals should be clearly marked. Where several dolls are to be made, it is quicker to draw one sheet only of squares and use tracing paper to copy the patterns on to.

As each pattern is copied, mark in the relevant details such as 'arm, cut 4', 'leave opening for stuffing' and seam allowances. In cases where there is more than one doll, mark this in also (e.g. 'father's leg, cut 4'), to avoid confusion later. Numbers in a circle on patterns indicate how many pieces to cut.

Check all patterns of garments against the doll before cutting out, as the shape of the doll's body may have altered slightly due to some fabrics stretching more than others or because of slight discrepancies in drawing the pattern.

Cutting out

Lay all pattern pieces on the wrong side of the required fabric, doubled if more than one piece of each is required. Draw round patterns on to fabric with a soft pencil, or tailor's chalk if the fabric is a dark colour. Or, if you prefer, pin pattern pieces on to fabric. Mark openings for stuffing, etc., and cut out, allowing for seams where required.

As a general rule in dressmaking, the centre front and back of a garment should be on the straight grain of the fabric and linings are cut on the bias. This applies also to doll-making, and does help clothes to hang correctly; but it is only really important if you are using a woven fabric such as wool, or a pattern—such as a stripe or check—which would look distinctly odd at an angle. The appearance of a dress can also be improved by, say, cutting the sleeves on the horizontal straight and the dress on the vertical, where this gives a contrast in the pattern.

Making up

If you are not an experienced dressmaker, it is advisable to pin and baste pieces together before sewing. This way it is easier to rectify mistakes at an early stage, and helps accuracy. It is, however, mentioned in the text only where it is more or less essential.

Generally speaking, machine-stitching is better than hand-stitching, particularly where any strain is put on the fabric as in the case of the dolls' bodies. But because the scale of the clothes is so small, there are places where it is almost impossible to use a machine: for instance, sewing a set-in sleeve to a bodice armhole, or even a bodice to a skirt. As most dolls are subjected to a lot of wear and tear, it is important that the sewing, whether by hand or machine, can stand a certain amount of strain.

Pressing seams as you go along is helpful; it is important where a second line of stitching is to cross a previous join, for instance when sewing together the inner leg seams of a pair of trousers or pants.

Trimming seams can also be important, particularly at sharp angles—round feet and hands, under arms of glove puppets, the points of a jester's hat. Several V-shaped notches, on curved seams, will help to avoid puckering.

The better a garment is finished the longer it is likely to last. On the other hand, making a doll should be an enjoyable experience, not a tedious chore. It is arguable whether it is better to produce one perfect example or several less perfect ones, particularly if you have an impatient would-be owner at your elbow.

If, therefore, you have chosen a non-fraying fabric, there is no need to oversew all the seams; you can use pinking shears. If you don't have any, you could at a pinch leave them as they are. A sewing machine that does zig-zag stitching is of course a boon here.

Machine-stitching can save time in several ways. If a dress is to have trimming round the skirt, the hem can be turned up and the trimming sewn on to the garment with the same line of stitching. You can also make a virtue out of white machine-stitching—as when sewing side seams or pockets to jeans, or, as in the case of the glove puppets in chapter 9, to accentuate the different colours at the same time as sewing them together. Hand-sewing on the other hand is best concealed unless the sewing is impeccably neat.

Because of the small scale of the work, it is easier to use bias binding to neaten armholes and necklines, rather than facing of the same fabric, or making a hem. This is done by sewing the bias binding, right sides facing, to the outside of the fabric at the sewing line, trimming the fabric seam if necessary, then bringing the binding over the seam to the inside of the garment, pressing or tacking (basting) it, and finally sewing it as you would a hem.

Fastenings

Snap fasteners are recommended throughout the book, because children find them easier to cope with than buttons, or hooks and eyes, or zippers. At the same time they are easier and quicker to sew on. Where buttons have been used these have been sewn to the front of the opening as decoration. There is no reasons why zippers or buttonholes should not be used instead if you wish. It is also possible to use Velcro, but it tends to be a little bulky used in such small areas.

Stuffing

Whatever stuffing is used for the bodies (see page 5), it should be inserted in small quantities at a time, starting with the furthermost corners, e.g. the head, or the toes and fingers, and working it well in—this is where the blunt end of a knitting needle comes in useful—and making sure it is really firm. It is always a surprise how much stuffing goes into one small doll. There are cases when a softer, less-filled look is needed, but on the whole really firm stuffing is best.

The finished look

The hair and features play an important part in the finished look of a doll (see chapter 2), but trimmings and accessories are important too. Used with discretion a trimming can make a dress look just right, but on the other hand a disproportionate amount or an ill-chosen one can spoil the whole effect. They are also useful for another reason: lace sewn round the neck and wrists of a doll's dress not only looks very pretty, it is also much easier to do than a collar and cuffs. Different accessories used with the same basic dress can entirely change its character, and there are so many to choose from that the possibilities are endless.

A look in the oddments box and around the house might produce some good results. Hoarders are at an advantage here. Decorative buttons make good brooches or pendants. A cameo can be made by sticking a circular piece of coloured felt on to a gold or black button, and then a second head-shaped piece on top. The button can first be sewn on to a choker ribbon. Shoe or watch-strap buckles can be used with velvet or petersham ribbon to make belts; an old leather belt can be cut down for the same purpose. A feather duster will provide enough feathers for a large number of Indian head-dresses, and the coloured variety is particularly good for decorating a Victorian hat, as are artificial flowers (see hats, chapter 2). Pretty necklaces can be made with beads, or from a watch chain, or even with small split curtain rings.

The important thing is to use the right accessories in the right colours, and only in moderation: to accentuate rather than obliterate. A word of warning: if the doll you are making is intended for a household with very young children, don't include anything that can be chewed off and swallowed, or that could hurt.

2 Hair and features, and hats

Hair

There are many methods of making dolls' hair, but quite a number of varied styles can be made from just one or two basic methods. The following is a guide to the ones used in this book. Amounts needed, ply thickness, lengths, etc., are given against individual dolls in each chapter.

It is advisable to cut the lengths of wool (yarn) slightly longer than you need so that the ends can be trimmed neatly later without making the style too short. As with people, a doll's character can change with her hairstyle—pulled well back from the face she will look older, a fringe and bunches will make her look younger. In methods 1, 2 and 3 the wool is sewn to the top of the head, and although the variations imitate real hairstyles, it is as well to remember that on people hair grows all over the head, not just at the parting, and that the latter restricts the possibilities. Catch-stitching the wool to the doll's head at strategic points can help to counteract this difference.

The wool should always be sewn firmly to the head, not to the wool underneath where there is more than one layer, or where there is a bun, otherwise it will soon come undone.

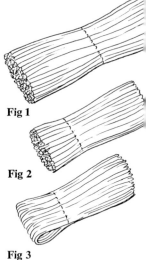

Fig 1

Fig 2

Fig 3

Method 1

Cut a number of lengths of wool (yarn). Sew across middle (fig. 1), preferably with a sewing machine (or the wool can be sewn to a ribbon or tape underneath). This line of stitching keeps the wool together before sewing to the head, and also forms the centre parting: the width varies (anything from $1\frac{1}{2}$ in. to 5 in.) depending on how far down the back you want the parting to go. Place hair-piece across head, slightly in front of seam, and sew to head along centre parting (fig. 4).

An alternative method of cutting the lengths is to wind wool round a piece of card measuring the required length (one full wind equals two lengths), remove from card, sew across middle and then cut through the loops. In some cases (see below, and for Baby in chapter 4) the loops can be left uncut.

Styles using method 1

Long hair (fig. 5): Arrange wool round head and stitch to head at ear level to keep in place. Trim ends.

Short hair (fig. 6): As long hair, but trimmed shorter.

Bunches (fig. 7): Gather in bunches either side of face and fasten by winding matching thread round and round, then stitching through several times. Make sure the bunches drape at the back (fig. 8), otherwise the hairstyle is too severe and leaves too much bare head. Stitch wool to head at ear level where necessary.

Plaits (braids): Plait wool on either side of head, starting at about ear level. Fasten ends by winding thread round as for bunches and stitch to head at ear level. Trim ends.

Method 2

This is method 1 with the addition of a fringe (bangs). Cut a number of lengths of wool and sew across about $2\frac{1}{2}$ in. to 3 in. from end (fig. 2). Lay over head with the short (fringe) end at front and sew to head at seam (fig. 9). Lay method 1 hair-piece over it at right angles (fig. 10) and proceed as above. The centre

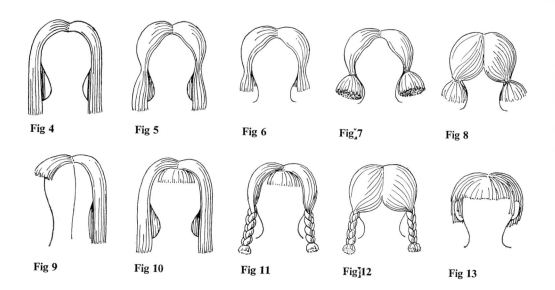

Fig 4   Fig 5   Fig 6   Fig 7   Fig 8

Fig 9   Fig 10   Fig 11   Fig 12   Fig 13

parting on the method 1 piece can be narrower here, as the back of the head is covered by the wool from the fringe-piece.

Styles using method 2

Long hair: As for method 1.

Short hair: As for method 1.

Plaits (braids) (figs 11 and 12): Divide wool in half at centre back. Bring each half round to side, and plait (braid). Proceed as method 1.

Bunches: Divide wool in half at centre back and proceed as method 1.

Boy's or man's hair (fig. 13): Make in the same way as for short hair above, but the fringe (bangs) should be wider and the wool cut in layers to make a good shape, rather than all one length.

Pony tail (fig. 14): Arrange wool round head. Bring a section from either side at front round and up to the back. Tie with a ribbon (or elastic band) to make pony tail. Stitch the remaining wool round the head at ear level and trim.

Pony tail and loop fringe (fig. 15): This is the style used in chapter 7 for the Victorian girls. It is a slight variation of method 2 in that the fringe piece is sewn on *after* the other piece. Proceed as for method 1, long hair. Make the fringe piece by winding wool round a piece of card to the length required (see above). Remove from card, sew across 3 in. from one end. Cut through loops at long end only (fig. 3). Now sew to head slightly to the *back* of head seam and tie ribbon round long ends to make pony tail.

Fig 14

Fig 15

Method 3

(*a*) Cut lengths and sew across middle as in method 1. Lay over head from front to back, and sew to head at hairline—i.e. forward from seam (fig. 16). Bring forward-falling hair back (fig. 17).

(*b*) Instead of sewing across middle, sew across with one end measuring the length of hairline to nape of neck (fig. 21). Place over head and proceed as for (*a*). This variation is useful where too much wool in a bun would overweight it but thickness generally is required.

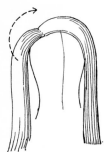

Fig 16

Fig 17

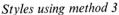

Fig 18

Fig 19

Fig 20

Styles using method 3

Top bun: Using 3(*a*), arrange wool round head, and stitch *all* lengths to head at or below ear level (fig. 18). Bring loose ends up to top of head and twist into bun shape. With matching wool sew firmly to head, tucking in all loose ends (fig. 19).

Pony tail (fig. 20): Using 3(*a*), proceed as for bun, but instead of twisting into shape, tie a ribbon round at the top to form a pony tail.

Back bun: Using 3(*b*), sew short ends to head (fig. 21). Bring long wool back and round to nape of neck. Twist into bun shape and sew firmly to head, tucking in stray ends (fig. 22). Catch stitch wool to head at ears and where necessary.

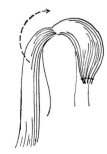

Fig 21

Method 4

Using single or double thickness of wool and a sharp-pointed needle, sew loops all over head (fig. 23), knotting at every fourth or sixth stitch so that the sewing does not come undone. The loops can be long or short, depending on what is required, and they can also be used for making beards or moustaches. This method is recommended especially for soft stretchy fabrics—such as the sock dolls in chapter 3—and for small or miniature dolls, particularly those made of felt.

Fig 22

Method 5

(*a*) Sew long wool stitches from top of head to ear level (fig. 24) round head.

(*b*) Alternatively, sew a row of stitches round back of head from ear to ear, and a couple of stitches at top of head, and weave wool between these stitches until head is covered (fig. 25).

Either of these methods can be used for small or miniature dolls, finger puppets, etc. Combined with loops, buns, etc., almost any style can be contrived.

Styles using method 5

Bearded man (fig. 26): Sew hair as (*a*) or (*b*). Sew loops as in method 4 round chin from ear to ear.

Moustached man (fig. 27): Sew hair as (*a*) or (*b*). Sew loops as in method 4 between nose and mouth to make moustache.

Period lady (figs 28 and 29): Sew hair as (*a*) or (*b*), then sew loops at either side at ear level. Bring needle out at top of head. Wind several small loops of wool together, place on head and sew round and through loops to make small bun, simultaneously sewing bun firmly to head.

Ringlets (figs 30 and 31): Sew several loops at front to make fringe (bangs), then sew hair as (*a*) or (*b*). Sew long loops all round from ear to ear.

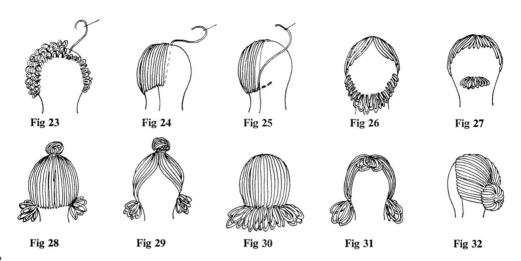

| Fig 23 | Fig 24 | Fig 25 | Fig 26 | Fig 27 |

| Fig 28 | Fig 29 | Fig 30 | Fig 31 | Fig 32 |

Bun (fig. 32): Sew long wool stitches (*a*) from front hairline to nape of neck. Wind several small loops round your little finger, place at back of head and sew round and through centre of loops to form a bun. Sew firmly to head.

Features

There is a narrow division between a face that looks right and a face that looks wrong: it may only be a slight difference in the width of the eyes or the relationship of the mouth to the nose, but—as with people—the whole character is changed. For this reason a 'dry run' is important to enable you to move the cut-out features about to find the best expression. Mouths are particularly difficult—there is only a small difference between a smile, a smirk and a pout. For embroidered faces, draw the features on a piece of tracing paper and place on face (or cut out similar shapes in felt as a guide). Patterns that tell you to embroider the face before sewing and stuffing the body can lead to some odd results as faces look very different before and after stuffing. As a general guide, features placed low on the face and close together will look younger than features higher up and wider apart.

Felt
Felt colours are clear and strong, and features made from felt have an immediate impact. Quite small squares of felt can be bought, so it need not be expensive, and it can either be glued or sewn on. Use glue very sparingly, otherwise it may show through the fabric. Always use sharp scissors, and try to avoid very thin strips or corners as these may start to fluff and break off.

Embroidery
Most embroidery threads are suitable, and a fine sharp needle is necessary. Wool (yarn) can be used occasionally, as for clown's eyes (crosses) or a mouth. Start by sewing through from the back of the head, so that the knot is hidden by hair.

The basic stitches used in embroidering features are shown in fig. 33. From the top, they are: satin stitch, straight stitch used here to make a star, running stitch returned to make a continuous line, outline stitch, chain stitch and french knot.

Eyes
Fig. 34 shows a selection of possible eyes. Left column: felt circle and felt eyebrow; felt circle on white felt oval with eyebrow in outline stitch; felt circle on

white felt oval outlined with double-thickness chain stitch. Right column: woollen cross for clown; felt circle sewn with eight-point star; felt circle on white oval outlined with single-thickness chain stitch and straight stitch eyelashes; embroidered satin stitch circle.

Noses
Fig. 35 shows a selection of noses. The top six are various shapes cut out of felt. The third row shows a satin stitch triangle and circle and two french knots (for nostrils). The three-dimensional bulbous nose is made of a large circle of felt, gathered round the outer edge and the resulting bag stuffed with a little kapok or cottonwool (absorbent cotton). It is then sewn to the face. This nose is particularly good for clown-like figures (see jester in chapter 6).

Mouths
Fig. 36 shows a selection of mouths. From top left: four shapes cut out of felt; embroidered mouth in outline stitch; embroidered mouth in chain stitch; two embroidered mouths in satin stitch.

Cheeks
These can be small circles or triangles cut out of felt, or stars made by sewing three or four straight stitches across each other—i.e. six- or eight-point stars—in pink embroidery thread. Round cheeks can also be made by embroidering a round spiral of running stitches, close together in the centre and gradually becoming wider apart towards the edge.

Beards and moustaches
These can be sewn with wool loops (see Hair, above) or cut out of felt and glued or sewn on.

Hats

Dolls' hats tend to get lost early in a doll's life, but sometimes they are necessary to identify a character. The drawings here are a general guide to the making of simple hats (not including those fully described and drawn elsewhere in the book). Felt is a useful material for hats. It needs no finished edges and it can easily be glued. For top hats, Welsh hats, etc., there is a thicker felt called flooring felt which needs no other stiffening but is heavier and difficult to work with. Fine buckram or canvas can be used to stiffen thinner materials; so can petersham ribbon. For miniature dolls, thin cardboard could also be used.

To make sure a hat fits properly, first cut the pattern pieces out of newspaper or cardboard and try them for size. Even a small difference is liable to make the hat sit on top of the head or fall over the eyes. To get the correct diameter measurement for a crown, the following is useful: measure the circumference of the head, multiply by 7 and divide by 22. The result is the length of the diameter from which to draw a circle for the crown.

Construction
Fig. 37 shows some basic construction methods for a variety of hats, which can be adapted as necessary.

A coolie hat is made by cutting the radius of circle A, and joining the two resulting cut ends over each other to form a shallow cone.

A shallow-crowned hat is made with brim B and crown C which is curved by means of three small darts at outer edge. Brim B is made in the same way as A,

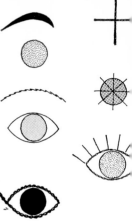

Fig 34

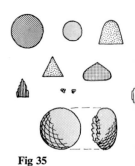

Fig 35

Fig 36

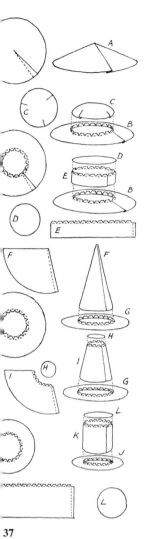

with the middle cut out and leaving a V-notched seam for joining to crown. For a higher crown, team B with side piece E and flat crown D.

The witch's hat is made with a flat brim (G) joined to a cone (F) which is made from a section of a circle. The Welsh hat is made in the same way but without a point, joining G to I and adding crown H. The top hat uses a flat brim (J), a high rectangular side piece (K) and flat crown (L).

The V-notched seam technique can be used with most medium thickness fabrics, or with thin cardboard, either by gluing or sewing.

The finished hats in fig. 38 illustrate the various ways of decorating different hats, using lace, ribbon, trimmings and feathers, etc.

Foot note

All the shoes in this book are made in the same way (with a slight variation in chapter 11). The shoe pattern is cut out of double thickness felt, then with right sides facing the shoe is sewn round the edge from heel to toe, trimmed and turned right side out. It can then be left as it is or decorated with felt or ribbon buckles.

37

Fig 38

3 Sock dolls

Socks are a useful and ready-made basis for a number of toys. The whole sock can be made into a hobby horse. With a few alterations, you can make a dog or a hedgehog, or a glove puppet. A sock can also be made into a very good cuddly doll.

Most kinds of sock are suitable, though some nylon or terylene socks tend to run and these should be avoided as they will start to come undone as soon as you cut them. An old sock is not only more economical, it also means there is no maker's name and size number to wash or rub off the sole! Even a darn in the toe can be hidden by the doll's hair. A medium-sized man's ankle sock makes a chubby doll. A calf-length sock will make a taller doll with longer arms and legs. The examples illustrated here have features made from buttons and felt, but if the doll is intended for a small child likely to put things into its mouth it would be safer to embroider the features or use only sewn-on felt.

Sizes of sock differ widely and some stretch more than others when stuffed. It is therefore important to check carefully the width and length of the dress pattern against the finished body before cutting out the dress. (This pattern is really only a guide to the shape of the dress, and is based on the medium ankle-length doll.)

Short doll (about 10 in. high)

Materials
One medium-sized dark brown man's ankle sock; $\frac{1}{2}$ lb kapok; $\frac{1}{2}$ oz black double-knitting wool (yarn); $\frac{1}{4}$ yd gingham or other cotton; 2 white buttons (approximately $\frac{2}{3}$ in.); scraps of black, red and pink felt; darning needle; 2 snap fasteners.

To make
Body: Cut sock in half at ankle and at lines indicated for arms and legs (fig. 39); the foot thus becomes the head and trunk of the doll, the leg is cut in four to make the doll's arms and legs (with the legs slightly longer than the arms). Start stuffing the body at the toe end, i.e. the doll's head. When you have stuffed to slightly below the dotted line in fig. 39, sew a double line of medium-sized stitching with brown cotton thread round the neck and pull tight like a draw-string (fig. 40), enough to emphasize the neckline but not so as to almost sever the head from the body. Fasten off and stitch through several times to make sure the stitching doesn't come undone.

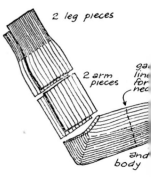

Fig 39

Continue to stuff until body is firm. Using the smooth sole as the front of the doll, take the open heel, turn the raw edge under, pull over and sew neatly.

With wrong side facing, sew arm and leg seams, leaving top end open for stuffing and rounding off the corners at other end (fig. 41). Turn right side out and stuff well. Turn top raw edges in neatly and sew together. With seams at back, sew arms to body at shoulder, legs slightly apart at hips (fig. 42).
Dress: Draw pattern pieces (pattern no. 1) on 1-in. squared paper (see page 7). Check against doll to make sure it is correct in width and length, and adjust as necessary. Cut out and draw round on to double thickness fabric. Cut out fabric, allowing $\frac{1}{4}$-in. seams. With right sides facing sew front lining to front dress, back lining to back dress (fig. 43). Trim sewn seams to $\frac{1}{8}$ in. and turn right side out. Press. With front and back of dress facing, sew side seams together. Neaten side seams. Turn right side out. Sew snap fasteners to shoulder openings. Try dress on doll and check length before turning hem under and sewing.

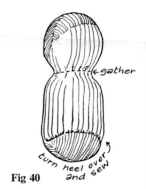

Fig 40

16

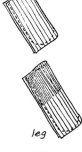

arm

leg

Fig 41

Fig 42

Hair: Using double thickness of wool (yarn) and a darning needle, sew short loops all over back and sides of the head, making a knot about every six stitches to prevent the wool being pulled out.

Features: Cut out two black felt circles to fit into the white buttons. Sew felt and buttons to face with black thread. Cut a small pink circle of felt for the nose and a red felt mouth and sew to face.

Tall doll (about 14 in. high)

Materials

One large beige man's calf-length sock; $\frac{1}{2}$ lb kapok; $\frac{1}{2}$ oz yellow double-knitting wool (yarn); $\frac{1}{2}$ yd patterned cotton; $\frac{3}{4}$ yd white trimming; 2 white buttons as above; scraps of brown, red and pink felt; darning needle; 2 snap fasteners.

To make

Proceed as for the smaller doll above. The arms and legs will be much longer, and the body is also longer in proportion. Alter the length and possibly the width of the dress pattern to fit the larger body. Sew white trimming to skirt hem. Make a neat hem all round the triangular scarf.

Further suggestions

Any of the hairstyles in chapter 2 can be adapted to suit this doll. The dress is very simple, to go with a simple-to-make doll. It can be trimmed with lace, ribbon or broderie-anglaise, and pockets, buttons or an apron added.

Fig 43

4 One-pattern dolls

The simplest way to make a fabric doll is to cut a shape out of a double thickness of material, sew round the edge leaving an opening, turn right side out and stuff. This was the basic principle used for the printed rag dolls sold in sheet form, first introduced at the turn of the century and recently revived. They were printed on cotton or linen and the designs ranged from dolls in full dress or only underwear to soldiers, sailors and animals. Some of them can be seen in the Bethnal Green Museum, London, and a few of the designs have been reprinted and can be bought there or from the Victoria and Albert Museum, London.

Any adult or child who can use a needle and thread reasonably well can make this kind of doll. Such an unsophisticated design has a certain number of drawbacks, the main one being that the arms and legs cannot be bent, so that the doll is perpetually standing. The patterns here have been kept on the small side, as large dolls made in this way become unwieldy.

Jack and Jill are made from flesh-coloured fabric and have removable clothes. The clown and guardsman's clothes are an integral part of the doll and the front and back body pieces are assembled separately before being sewn together. The clown is made from a striped fabric with a piece of white sewn on for the face, the guardsman is made of felt with the traditional black busby, black trousers and red jacket.

Jack and Jill (about 14 in. high)

Materials
½ yd flesh-coloured cotton poplin, calico or similar fabric; 1 lb kapok; 1 oz double-knitting wool (yarn); snap fasteners; felt scraps for features; bias binding. For Jack: ¼ yd plain cotton (trousers), ¼ yd patterned cotton (shirt). For Jill: ¼ yd plain cotton (blouse), ¼ yd patterned cotton (skirt), to match or contrast with Jack's clothes.

To make
Draw pattern pieces (pattern no. 1) on to 1-in. squared paper. Cut out and place on appropriate fabrics (double thickness). Draw round and cut out leaving ⅓-in. seam allowance except where indicated.
Bodies: With right sides facing, sew front and back body together, leaving opening for stuffing as shown on pattern (fig. 44). Trim seams neatly, particularly at narrow curves under arms, between legs and round head, hands and feet (fig. 45). Turn right side out and stuff well, starting with head, hands and feet. Sew up opening neatly.
Hair: For Jill, cut 26 lengths of wool (yarn), 10 in. long. Sew across, 2½ in. from one end, then sew wool to head horizontally along this seam, so that the short end forms the fringe (bangs). Cut 60 lengths, 15 in. long. Sew across centre, place over fringe piece and sew to head along parting. (See page 11 for diagrams.) Plait into two plaits (braids) and fasten by winding round the ends with matching cotton thread, then stitching through several times. Trim ends. Sew to head at ear level to keep in place.

For Jack, cut 26 lengths, 8 in. long, leaving 2½ in. for fringe as above, and 60 lengths, 11 in. long. Proceed as above (except for plaits!) and trim to required length.
Features: Cut out circles of blue or brown felt for eyes, pink triangle for nose,

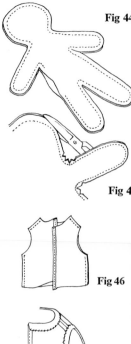

Fig 44

Fig 4

Fig 46

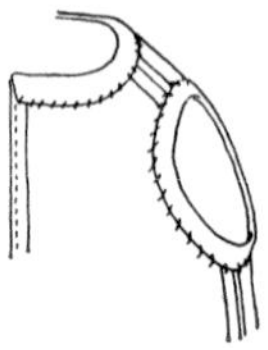

Fig 47

18

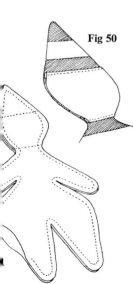

red crescent for mouth and small dark pink circles for cheeks, and glue or sew on to face.

Blouse/shirt: With right sides facing, sew front to back at side seams and shoulders. Turn in back openings and sew (fig. 46). Trim and press seams. Turn bottom hem under and sew. Using bias binding, neaten armholes and neck. In the illustration Jack's shirt has white bias binding turned over neck opening and sewn to right side of fabric to form a contrasting collar. Jill's neck opening is left plain, with the bias binding stitched neatly to the underside (fig. 47). Sew snap fasteners to back opening.

Jill's skirt: With right sides facing, sew front and back together at side seams. Trim seams. Turn in at waist and sew. The straps can be made in one of two ways (fig. 48): either fold in half and sew together on the wrong side, turning them right side out by easing one end through the resultant tube with a crochet hook, or needle and thread; or turn in one edge, place over the other edge and sew together on the right side. Press straps and skirt seams. Turn strap ends in and sew to neaten. Sew straps to inside of front and back skirt, crossing them over at the back. Snap fasteners could be sewn at back for easier taking off. Check hem length, turn in and sew.

Jack's trousers: With right sides facing, join centre seams front and back. Trim seams and press open. Sew front to back along inside leg curve (fig. 49). Turn right side out. Turn in waist and sew. Make straps as for Jill's skirt and fasten to trousers in the same way. Check leg length, turn in trouser bottoms and sew.

Clown

Materials

½ yd striped or other cotton, linen, polyester/cotton mixture or similar (this fabric needs to be strong and not too light in colour as there are no removable clothes and it is likely to get some pretty hard wear); small piece of white cotton or unbleached calico; orange wool (yarn) for hair; length of black wool (yarn) for eyes; 9-in. square of white felt for ruff and buttons; scraps of pink and red felt; ½ lb kapok.

To make

Draw pattern pieces (pattern no. 2) on to 1-in. squared paper, cut out and draw round on double thickness fabric, marking in the sewing line for face. Cut out, allowing ⅓-in. seam. Turn top and bottom of face piece in, place on right side of front body and sew along lines indicated (fig. 50). Cut away body material behind face to avoid puckering later. With right sides facing, sew front body to back body, leaving opening for stuffing (fig. 51). Trim seams carefully, particularly round curves, turn right side out and stuff firmly. Sew up opening.

Hair: With orange wool, sew loops approximately 1½ in. long to hat at either side of face.

Features: With black wool sew two large crosses for eyes. Cut large pink felt circle for nose, wide red crescent for mouth, and glue or sew on.

Ruff: Pull circle over head and position at neck. Sew a line of gathering stitches round inner rim and pull thread until the circumference fits that of the neck. Fasten, and sew ruff to neck. Glue or sew on buttons to front body and hat.

Guardsman

Materials

¼ yd black felt; a 12-in. square or ¼ yd red felt; white felt for hands and trimming; scraps of felt for features, including yellow for buckle; gold braid; 1 yd narrow white braid; ½ lb kapok. (Felt is the best fabric for this doll because the edges can be left raw. If other material is used allow for seams.)

To make

Draw pattern pieces (pattern no. 3) on to 1-in. squared paper, cut out and draw round on appropriate coloured felt. Cut out, leaving ⅓-in. seams only where indicated. Use white thread if machine-sewing. Sew front busby to face, inserting ends of gold braid as fig. 52. Sew front jacket to neck and trouser waist at indicated sewing line, and hands to wrist. Repeat at back—sewing busby to jacket at neck. With right sides facing, sew front body to back body leaving an opening for stuffing. Trim seams neatly and turn right side out. Stuff firmly. Sew up opening. Sew black band round neck and black cuffs to wrists. Sew white piping to top of neckband and cuffs and down front of red jacket. Sew white belt round waist, covering up line of stitching, and glue or sew two strips and a circle of yellow felt to the belt to make the buckle. Glue or sew on eyes, nose and mouth.

Further suggestions (see drawing on title page)

Chinaman: Make out of felt as for guardsman, but using Jack's head shape. The jacket could be turquoise with a white collar and cuffs, the trousers navy or other dark colour. The black hair is like Jill's but longer and of thinner wool (yarn). It is plaited (braided) in one piece at the back of the head. The hat is made of a circle of fine buckram or canvas with a slit cut from the circumference to the centre, and one of the resultant edges slid over the other to form a shallow cone (see page 15). Tie to head with a narrow ribbon sewn to inside of cone.

Hula girl: Make as for Jill, but using a brown fabric and black wool for hair, which is left loose (with catch stitching all round at ear level to keep in place). The grass skirt is made of a piece of straw-coloured felt, the width corresponding to Jill's skirt length, the length equalling twice the doll's waist measurement. With a sharp pair of scissors cut into strips, leaving a narrow band along one edge. Wind twice round the doll and stitch together. Turn band under to give flounce and stitch to body. Alternatively the grass skirt could be made out of raffia.

The *lei* can be made of flower-shaped circles of different coloured felt strung on to nylon or button thread, and the flower behind her ear could also be made of felt.

Clown No. 2: Make as Chinaman, using pink for head and hands, white for shirt (jacket pattern) and collar, and black for legs (trouser pattern). Make checked trousers as for Jack, but wider at either side to make them baggy. Add a patterned ribbon for a floppy tie and a black felt top hat made of two circles and a rect-angle (see page 15). The eyelids are semicircles of white felt, the bulbous nose is made like the jester's in chapter 6 (page 29).

Father Christmas: Make as Chinaman, using pink for head and hands, red for jacket, black for trousers and white for cuffs (no collar). The red hood is made as the one for the baby in chapter 5, plus a white trim. Add a white strip down centre front and a white belt as for the guardsman but with a black square buckle. To make his coat longer (as in the illustration) you can sew a horizontal band of red felt to the basic jacket, after stuffing but before adding trimming and belt, and hide the join with the belt. Use white wool for hair and beard, which could be sewn in loops.

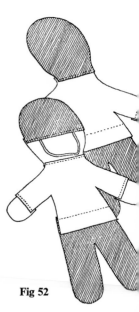

Fig 52

5 Single-hinge dolls

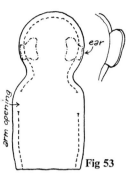

Fig 53

This type of doll, though still simple to make, has separate arms and legs to allow for a certain amount of movement and enable the doll to be sat down. It is also easier to dress and undress. The head and body are in one piece and it is important to stuff the doll very firmly, particularly round the neck, otherwise the head tends to flop. The father, mother and twins are made from the same basic pattern—with length differences in the body, arms and legs. The baby has its own pattern, as its head is also smaller, but is made in the same way. Father and son have ears to make them look more realistic: they both have knitted polo-neck sweaters. Mother has a simple long-sleeved dress and white petticoat and pants. The daughter has a slightly more complicated dress with matching pants, and the baby is wearing a one-piece sleep suit.

Basic doll

Materials

$\frac{1}{3}$ yd flesh-coloured cotton poplin, flannelette, calico or similar fabric; 1 lb of kapok; felt scraps for eyes, nose, mouth and cheeks. Approximate heights: father 21 in., mother 20 in., twins 16 in., baby 11 in.

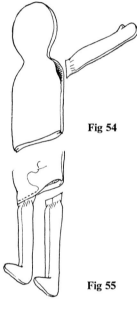

Fig 54

Fig 55

To make

Draw pattern pieces (pattern no. 4) on to 1-in. squared paper, using appropriate body, arm and leg measurements, and including ears for father and son. Cut out and place on double thickness fabric. Draw round, marking arm and ear openings on body. Allowing $\frac{1}{3}$-in. seam except where indicated, cut out fabric. With right sides facing, sew body—including ears for father and son (see below) —leaving openings for arms and at base for stuffing (fig. 53). Turn right side out. With right sides facing, sew arms and legs leaving tops open for stuffing. Trim all sewn seams neatly, particularly inside curves and round thumbs and toes. Turn right sides out. Stuff arms firmly, starting with thumbs. Turn in shoulder seam openings on body and insert top of arms, thumbs upward (fig. 54). Pin, then sew together neatly.

Stuff body well, making sure there is ample stuffing in neck to avoid flopping. Stuff legs, starting with toes. Turn in seam allowance at base of body, insert legs (toes front) and stitch across (figs. 55 and 56). A double row of stitches will ensure that the doll sits easily. Note that leg seams are at centre front, arm seams at side.

Ears: The ears, made of a double thickness of material, are included when stitching the body (father or son) together. With right sides facing, stitch pairs of ear pieces together, leaving the inside curve open. Trim and turn right side out. Place ears between front and back body pieces as marked and *ease* in so that curves correspond (fig. 53). Pin or tack (baste). Now proceed to sew round body as above.

Features (best done after the addition of hair—see below): Cut blue or brown felt circles for eyes, pink triangles or circles for nose, red for mouth and dark pink circles for cheeks. Sew eyes with matching thread to face with an eight-point star. With pink thread sew on nose, and (with a six-point star) the cheeks. Sew mouth on with red thread. Alternatively the nose and mouth can be glued on with Copydex (Sobo). Even when sewing on the features, it helps to glue the felt lightly to the face first.

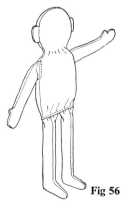

Fig 56

21

Father or son

Materials

As for basic doll (page 21), plus: $\frac{1}{2}$ oz double-knitting wool (yarn) (brown for father, rust for son); 2–3 oz double-knitting wool (light brown for father, turquoise for son); 1 pair each No. 9 and 11 knitting needles; large safety pin or stitch holder; $\frac{1}{4}$ yd needlecord, denim, medium worsted or similar fabric (brown for Father, navy or grey for Son); snap fasteners; pieces of felt for shoes; felt scraps for features.

To make

Body: Make as basic body above, using measurements marked 'Father' or 'twins' and including ears.

Hair: Cut 100 lengths of wool (yarn), 8 in. long. Sew across $2\frac{1}{2}$ in. from one end. With this $2\frac{1}{2}$ in. as fringe (bangs), sew to top of head—the fringe should be roughly the same width as the face, wider than for a girl. Cut 60 lengths of 9-in. wool. Sew across middle. Place across fringe piece and sew to head down centre parting. Arrange round face, giving father sideboards with several pieces pulled forward in front of ears, and catch stitch to head at lower layer. Trim wool to give a good shape. (See chapter 2 for diagrams.) Sew or glue on features as above.

Knitted jumper: Abbreviations—st(s). = stitch(es); st.-st. = stocking stitch (one row knit, one row purl); K. = knit; P. = purl; tbl = through back of loops; tog. = together.

Figures in brackets refer to the smaller jumper for the Son.

BACK: With No. 11 needles cast on 32 (30) sts. Rib for 9 rows. Change to No. 9 needles and proceed in st.-st. for 3 (2) in. *Shape armholes:* Cast off 2 sts. at beg. of next two rows. *3rd row* K. *4th row* P. *5th row* K.1, K.2 tog., K. to last 3 sts., K.2 tog.tbl, K.1. *6th row* P. Repeat 3rd to 6th rows until 18 sts. remain. K. one row, P. one row. Slip remaining sts. on to large safety pin or stitch holder.

FRONT: As Back.

SLEEVES: With No. 11 needles cast on 26 sts. Rib for 7 rows. Change to No. 9 needles and proceed in st.-st. increasing 1 st. at beg. and end of 5th, 9th, 13th and (father only) 17th row, until length equals underarm measurement of doll. *Shape armholes:* Cast off 2 sts. at beg. of next two rows. *3rd row* K.1, K.2 tog., K. to last 3 sts., K.2 tog.tbl, K.1. *4th row* P. Repeat 3rd and 4th rows until 8 sts. remain. Slip remaining sts. on to safety pin or stitch holder. Repeat pattern for second sleeve.

NECK: Slip stitches on to No. 11 needle in the following order: left sleeve, front, right sleeve, back. Rejoin wool and rib for 9 rows. Cast off in ribbing.

TO MAKE UP: Press separate pieces lightly. Sew up underarm, side and shoulder seams, leaving neck open. Sew snap fasteners to neck opening.

Father's trousers: Draw pattern pieces (pattern no. 6) on 1-in. squared paper. Cut out and place on fabric. Draw round, and cut out allowing $\frac{1}{3}$-in. seams. Turn top edge of pockets under and stitch across. Turn other three sides under, place on right side of trouser back as illustrated (fig. 60) and sew to trousers on these three sides, leaving the previously sewn top as opening. With right sides facing, sew outer leg seams together. With right sides facing, sew back centre seams together, and front seams as far as indicated on pattern. Trim and press centre seams open at base. Sew inner leg seams from ankle to ankle (fig. 57). Trim curve, press and neaten all seams. Turn in ends of waistband and with right sides facing sew to top of trousers leaving front open (fig. 58). Trim seam, turn band over so that it is folded in half, and sew to inside of trousers (fig. 59). Sew

Fig 57 **Fig 58**

Fig 59

Fig 60

Fig 61

Fig 62 **Fig 63**

up open ends of band. Check length before turning trouser bottoms in, and hem. Sew on snap fasteners.

To make trousers look like jeans, use white machine-stitching to sew pockets (fig. 60), and sew a double line of white stitching down outer seams before joining centre seams.

Son's shorts: These are made in the same way as the trousers, but cut short as pattern.

Shoes: Cut out shoes in felt as pattern. With right sides facing, sew together in pairs, leaving top open. Trim seams and turn right side out.

Mother

Materials

As for basic doll (page 21), plus: 1 oz yellow or light brown double-knitting wool (yarn); ⅓ yd patterned or plain cotton or other dress fabric; ⅓ yd white nylon, lawn or similar lingerie fabric; 1 yd narrow lace trimming (optional); piece of felt matching dress for shoes; felt scraps for features; snap fasteners; narrow elastic.

To make

Body: Make as for basic body using measurements marked 'mother'.

Hair: Cut wool into 36-in. lengths, leaving enough for sewing with later. Sew across middle, then sew to top of head slightly in front of seam, so that half the wool falls forward over the face. Pull the forward-falling wool back and arrange round face. Catch stitch all round at ear level. Bring all the loose ends up and twist into a bun on top of the head, pushing in loose ends, and pin to hold in position. Sew bun to hair firmly with reserved length of wool. (For diagrams, see chapter 2.) Sew or glue on features as above.

Draw pattern pieces (pattern no. 4) on 1-in. squared paper. Cut out, place on appropriate fabric and draw round. Cut out allowing ⅓ in. seams except where indicated.

Dress: With right sides facing, sew side and shoulder seams of dress and under-arm seams of sleeves. With right sides facing, ease sleeves into dress at shoulders, pin and sew (fig. 61). Turn in back openings and sew. Collar: with right sides facing sew collar pieces together leaving inside curve open (fig. 62). Trim to ⅛ in., turn right side out and press. Turn seams on inner curve in towards each other and baste together. Sew the two collar pieces to inside neck of dress (fig. 63), from centre front to back opening. Neaten edge of dress under collar, trimming first if necessary. Turn collar down and press. Check length of dress on doll, then sew hem. Sew on snap fasteners to back opening.

Petticoat and pants: With right sides facing, sew side seams of petticoat. Neaten these seams. Turn hem in at waist, wide enough to take elastic, and sew leaving small opening. Insert elastic. Check length, turn in skirt hem and sew. Add lace trimming if required. With right sides facing, sew centre front and back seams of pants. Trim seams and press open. Sew inside leg curve. Turn in waist and leg openings and sew. Add lace trimming if required.

Shoes: Make as for father, adding strap by sewing to inside of shoe on either side.

Daughter

Materials

As for basic doll (page 21), plus: 1 oz rust-red double-knitting wool (yarn) to match boy twin; ½ yd flowered cotton, rayon, Vyella or similar fabric; ½ yd white trimming; narrow elastic; snap fasteners; piece of felt for shoes matching dress; felt scraps for features.

To make
Body: Make as for basic doll using measurements marked 'twins'.
Hair: Cut 70 lengths of wool, 10 in. long. Sew across 3 in. from one end. With this 3 in. as fringe (bangs), sew wool to head. Cut 100 lengths, 14 in. long, and sew across middle. Place across fringe-piece and sew to head down centre parting. Arrange in loose bunches either side of face and fasten by winding matching thread round ends and stitching through. Catch-stitch hair all round to head at ear level to keep in place. Trim ends to required length. Sew or glue on features as above.

Draw and cut out pattern no. 5. Place on double thickness fabric, draw round and cut out allowing $\frac{1}{3}$-in. seams except where indicated (note length of seam allowance on sleeves).

Dress: Gather top of skirt front to match width of bodice yoke *A* and join skirt to yoke with right sides facing (fig. 64). Do the same to each back piece. With right sides facing, join sleeves to skirt at *B* front and back. Join shoulders *C*, under-arms *D*, skirt *E*. Press and neaten seams and clip at corners to avoid rucking. Turn in wide seam on each sleeve and sew with two lines of stitches along lines indicated (fig. 65) leaving a small opening to insert elastic. Insert narrow elastic (fig. 66). (Alternatively a gathering line of shirring elastic can be used instead.) Turn in and hem centre back openings. Turn in and hem neck neatly, or use bias binding. Stitch on white trimming. Check length and sew skirt hem. Sew snap fasteners to back opening.

Matching pants: Join seams at centre front and back. Trim seams and press open. Sew inside leg curve. Turn in hem at waist and leg openings wide enough to allow for narrow elastic, and leave small openings. Insert elastic.

Shoes: Make as for mother.

Baby

Materials
As for basic doll, page 21 ($\frac{1}{4}$ yd is enough); $\frac{1}{2}$ oz yellow double-knitting wool (yarn); $\frac{1}{2}$ yd white towelling (terrycloth), brushed nylon or similar fabric; shirring elastic; white bias binding; snap fasteners; felt scraps for features.

To make
Body: Make as for basic doll, but using pattern no. 6 (body, arm and leg).
Hair: Wind 25 full turns round a piece of card $4\frac{1}{2}$ in. long. Take off card, sew across $1\frac{1}{2}$ in. from end. With this $1\frac{1}{2}$ in. as fringe (bangs), sew to head. Wind 25 full turns round a second card, 6 in. long. Take off card and sew across middle. Lay this over fringe-piece and sew to head down centre parting. Catch stitch to head all round to keep in place. Leaving the wool uncut in this way gives the baby a curly look, but alternatively the hair can be made as for the father using the above measurements. Sew or glue on features.
Sleep suit: Draw and cut out pattern no. 6 as above. With right sides facing, sew centre back seam, and centre front seam as far as marked on pattern. Trim at base and press seams open. With right sides facing sew front to back at shoulders, and from one underarm round both legs to the other underarm (fig. 67). With right sides facing, sew hood pieces together along back and top seams, then sew to neck of suit. Turn in hood and front opening and sew using bias binding. Neaten seams. If towelling (terrycloth) is used, bias binding can be used for

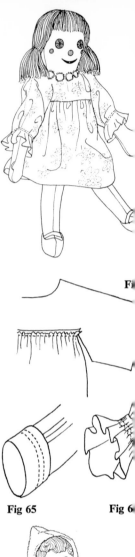

F

Fig 65   **Fig 6**

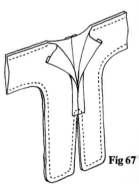

Fig 67

these too as this material frays easily. Turn in and hem sleeves at wrist. Run a line of stitches round each ankle, at line indicated on pattern, with shirring elastic to gather it in. Sew snap fasteners to front opening.

Further suggestions

Sailor: Using a basic body as for father, make the hair in the same way, but cut shorter. Make a vest from white cotton as bodice of mother's dress (but cut short) and trim with navy bias binding round the neck. The trousers can be made of navy cotton, using the father's trouser pattern, but flaring the legs to give bellbottoms. The top can be made of some stretch fabric (e.g. jersey) using the mother's dress pattern with the following alterations: sailor's back as mother's front; sailor's front as mother's front, but with a low V down the centre; side seams cut straight to fit. The collar is made as fig. 68 from a piece of light blue cotton with three rows of white machine-stitching on the outer edge. It is then tucked into the neck of the jersey, stitched to hold it in place and trimmed with a black ribbon at the front. The cap can be made of white felt (as fig. 68) cutting two equal circles, the lower one having a second inner circle cut out to fit top of head, but leaving a notched seam. With right sides facing, sew outer edge of circles together, trim and turn inside out. Sew inner rim to a $1\frac{1}{2}$-in. wide band with notched seam inside band. Trim band with navy petersham ribbon which will also stiffen it. The crown could also be stiffened with a circle of fine buckram sewn to the underside. For authenticity you could add a white cord lanyard and embroider the ship's name on the cap band.

Eskimo: Again make as father (with black hair). The clothes should be made of some thickish material (or they could be lined) in a stone or leather colour. The fabric should look as much like an animal skin as possible, i.e. not a weave. The trousers are made like father's. The jacket is made like mother's dress, but cut short and straightened at side seams, and with the opening at the front instead of the back. The hood is a slightly larger version of the baby's, sewn into the neck in the same way and trimmed with mock fur (which can be bought in narrow widths by the yard). The gloves could also be of fur, and the jacket could be embroidered round the cuffs and hem.

Note: If you cannot knit, father's jumper could be made instead from the sleeve of an old machine-knitted jersey, by cutting a whole section for the body, with slits at either side for the sleeves, cutting and making sleeves as for mother's dress, and hemming all raw edges carefully. If the cuff end of the sleeve is used, it can be turned over to make a polo-neck. The sailor's jersey can be adapted in the same way.

fig 68

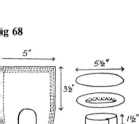

6   Double-hinge dolls

Fig 69

Fig 70

Fig 71

Based in principle on the traditional jointed doll, this doll has hinged elbows and knees as well as hinged shoulders and hips. The easy movement of arms and legs goes particularly well with a tall, lanky doll. The head is made separately out of four pieces, and sewn to the body before stuffing—both easier and stronger.

Mrs Moppety (an old-fashioned housekeeper or nanny figure) has a dress with inset puffed sleeves, a full gathered skirt and front opening with buttons. Her apron matches her mob cap. The peasant girl has a white puffed-sleeved blouse and apron and a black or dark-coloured dress and scarf. Her costume is not related to any specific country, but similar costumes can be found in many alpine regions in Europe. The jester is made of felt with a removable cap and tunic. Felt is best for the tunic because you need a non-fraying fabric for the dagged (zig-zag) hem, and for the cap because it needs to be rather stiff. The body could however be made up in cotton or other fabric as long as it matches the colour of the felt, but this is not always easy.

Basic doll (22 in. high)

Materials

½ yd skin-coloured cotton poplin, rayon, unbleached calico or similar fabric; 1 lb of kapok.

To make

Draw pattern pieces (pattern no. 7) on to 1-in. squared paper and cut out. Place on double thickness fabric and draw round. Cut out, leaving ⅓-in. seam allowance. With right sides facing, join head pieces at front and back centre seams. With right sides facing, join front head to front body across neck, and back head to back body (fig. 69). Trim sewn seams. Now sew front body and head to back body and head, leaving base open for stuffing. Trim and turn right side out. Stuff head and body firmly.

With right sides facing, sew arms and legs, leaving tops open for stuffing. Trim, particularly round hands and feet, and turn right side out. Stuff arms firmly, working well into thumbs, almost as far as dotted line indicated on pattern. Sew a line of stitching across to make joint. Note that seams should be at sides. Continue stuffing to second dotted line and sew another line of stitching across. Turn top seam in, sew together and sew to body horizontally at shoulders (fig. 70). Make sure thumbs face front.

Stuff legs in the same way as arms (this time seams should be at centre front and back). Turn in body seam at base and insert legs, making sure feet face front. Sew across base (fig. 71)—twice for firmness.

Mrs Moppety

Materials

Body as basic doll (see above); 1 oz double-knitting wool or dishcloth cotton (yarn); 1 yd striped, checked or floral cotton; 1 yd white or coloured cotton, cotton poplin or cotton/polyester mixture; 1 yd white broderie anglaise or lace trimming; snap fasteners; 4 small buttons to match dress; shirring elastic; matching felt for shoes; scraps for eyes and nose; embroidery thread.

Choose fabrics to complement each other: green and blue floral dress with blue apron and cap (and yellow hair), orange and white gingham dress with

Fig 72

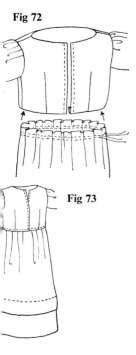

Fig 73

Fig 74

Fig 75

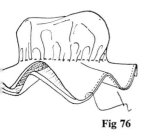

Fig 76

orange apron and cap (and brown hair), maroon, grey and white stripes with white apron and cap (and white hair).

To make
Body: Make basic body as above.
Hair: Cut 60 to 70 lengths, 20 in. long, of double-knitting wool or dish-cloth cotton (yarn), and sew across 6 in. from one end. Sew to head at forehead with the 6-in. piece towards the *back* and the long lengths falling over face. Take these longer lengths back and arrange round head, stitching at ear level to keep in place. Now pull them to the back, twist into a bun and sew to head firmly, tucking in wool ends as you go. (For diagrams, see page 12.)
Features: Stitch two round felt eyes to face with an eight-point star, sew on round pink nose. With red embroidery thread embroider mouth, using a narrow chain stitch or outline stitch.

Draw pattern pieces for clothes (pattern nos 7 and 8) on 1-in. squared paper; cut out in appropriate fabrics, allowing $\frac{1}{3}$-in. seams except where otherwise indicated—front bodice pattern allows $\frac{1}{3}$ in. overlap.
Dress: Make darts in front and back bodice as indicated on pattern. With right sides facing, join bodice sides and shoulders. Press seams and turn right side out. Turn in seam allowance at front openings, leaving enough for overlap, and sew. Sew a loose gathering stitch along top of each sleeve as indicated. Sew underarm seams. Pull gathering thread until opening matches bodice armhole, and knot. With right sides facing, pin sleeves to armholes and sew. With right sides facing, join skirt seam. Using two lines of gathering stitches, gather skirt at waist to correspond to bodice (fig. 72). Turn bodice seam under at waist—allow overlap at front opening—and pin to skirt (skirt seam at centre back). Sew together (fig. 73). Neaten seams. Turn neck and wrist seams under and sew. Sew on white trimming to neck and wrists. Turn up hem of skirt and sew. Make a tuck in the skirt to fall about 1$\frac{1}{2}$ in. from the hem (fig. 73), checking skirt length at the same time. Sew on snap fasteners to front opening, then buttons on front of overlap.
Apron: Turn in and sew side and hem seams. Turn waistband seams in and baste each separately (fig. 74). Fold in half lengthways. Gather top of apron slightly (to go about two-thirds way round waist) and place between waistband fold (fig. 75) leaving equal lengths of band for tying at back. Pin and/or baste. Stitch together whole length of waistband, including apron. Turn in open ends and sew. Sew white trimming to apron hem.
Mob cap: Place circles together and sew a double row of gathering stitches all round approximately 2$\frac{3}{4}$ in. from brim. This can be done with shirring elastic. Pull to gather until it fits head, then fasten—it is best left slightly on the loose side otherwise the cap tends to slip off the bun. Turn brim edges in towards each other and sew together neatly, very near the edge (fig. 76). A narrow ribbon matching the dress can be sewn over the gather to neaten the appearance.
Shoes: With right sides facing, sew shoe pieces (from pattern no. 9) together from heel to toe. Trim and turn right side out.

(Although pattern and instructions for petticoat and pants are not included here, these could be made using patterns given for the Victorian dolls in chapter 7, adjusting measurements where necessary.)

Peasant girl

Materials
Body as basic doll (page 26); 1 oz yellow double-knitting wool (yarn); $\frac{3}{4}$ yd plain black, spotted, floral or checked cotton or other dark-coloured fabric; $\frac{1}{2}$

yd white cotton or cotton/polyester mixture; 1 yd white broderie anglaise or lace trimming; $\frac{1}{2}$ yd machine-embroidered ribbon or braid (patterned with edelweiss, hearts or flowers); snap fasteners; white or pearl buttons; black bias binding; felt for shoes; scraps for eyes, nose, cheeks; red embroidery thread for mouth.

To make
Body: Make as for basic doll.
Hair: Cut 60 or 70 lengths of wool, 20 in. long. Sew across centre. Place horizontally on head, so that wool comes either side of face, and sew to head down parting. Make two plaits (braids) and fasten ends by winding round with yellow thread and stitching through several times. Catch stitch wool to head at ear level.
Features: Sew on features as for Mrs Moppety, but use small pink felt circles (darker than nose) for cheeks.

Draw pattern pieces (pattern nos 7 and 8) on 1-in. squared paper; cut out as above in appropriate fabrics, allowing $\frac{1}{3}$ in. for seams. Note that $\frac{1}{3}$ in. overlap is allowed for back blouse and front bodice openings.
Blouse: Make as Mrs Moppety's dress bodice, using sleeves marked 'peasant'. Neaten waist seam. Sew white trimming to neck and sleeves. When sewing trimming to sleeves, the sleeve ends should be slightly gathered. Sew on snap fasteners to back opening.
Dress: Make in same way as Mrs Moppety's, but without sleeves and using bodice pattern marked 'peasant' and correct length skirt, without tuck. Neaten armholes and neck with bias binding. Sew on snap fasteners and two buttons at front.
Apron: Make in same way as Mrs Moppety's, using the shorter pattern, but use embroidered ribbon or braid, instead of white waistband, and no ties. Fasten at back with a snap fastener.
Scarf: Hem neatly all round and press. Lay across head with right angle at centre back, bring other two corners back and over first corner and tie in knot (fig. 77).

(Again petticoat and pants can be made as in chapter 7, or as for mother in chapter 5.)
Shoes: As above.

Jester

Materials
$\frac{1}{2}$ yd each of blue and green felt (or purple and yellow, orange and red, or any other two contrasting colours); $\frac{1}{8}$ yd pink cotton, or felt; scraps of felt for features; 2 snap fasteners; kapok.

Fig 77

To make
Body: Make as for basic doll (page 26), using pink for head, blue for body, left arm and right leg, and green for right arm and left leg.

Draw patterns (pattern no. 9) for tunic and cap on 1-in. squared paper; cut out, allowing $\frac{1}{3}$-in. seams only where indicated. Felt edges are left raw, so the tunic neck, armholes, dagged hem, front of cap and collar can be left as cut—use sharp scissors for this. Check that you have cut out the right colours—two of each colour of top and bottom tunic pieces, one of each colour front and back cap and collar.
Tunic: With right sides facing, sew the blue top tunic pieces to the bottom green ones—these are the right-hand front and back. Sew the top green to the bottom

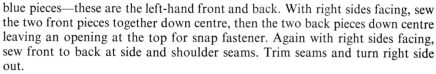

blue pieces—these are the left-hand front and back. With right sides facing, sew the two front pieces together down centre, then the two back pieces down centre leaving an opening at the top for snap fastener. Again with right sides facing, sew front to back at side and shoulder seams. Trim seams and turn right side out.

Cap: With right sides facing, sew the two back pieces together, and the two front pieces above face only (fig. 78). With right sides facing, sew front to back at sides. With right sides facing, join collar at back and sew to cap at neck, leaving front open. Trim seams, particularly at points, and turn right side out. Sew snap fasteners to cap at chin and to tunic at back opening.

N.B. None of this is really as complicated as it sounds, but to get the colours alternating correctly it is a good idea to check against the illustration as you go along.

Features: Cut two circles for eyes and glue or sew on. Cut a circle of dark pink or red felt about $1\frac{1}{2}$–$1\frac{3}{4}$ in. diameter, sew a gathering thread round outer edge, pull fairly tight and stuff with kapok to make a soft ball shape. Sew to centre of face. Cut out a wide crescent for mouth and pink triangles for cheeks and sew or glue on. You could add orange wool hair if you wish, made as for the father in chapter 5, or the clown puppet in chapter 9—but don't use too much wool, otherwise the cap may not fit.

Fig 78

Further suggestions

Gipsy: Make as for peasant girl, but with black hair and a fringe (bangs). The dress, of dark plain or patterned cotton, is a combination of Mrs Moppety's bodice plus the peasant's sleeves and skirt. She has a plain white apron with white ties, a red and white spotted head scarf and large brass curtain rings for ear-rings. Also a three-cornered shawl made of a soft material with a wool fringe —or knitted or crocheted.

Welsh girl: Make as for Mrs Moppety with brown hair. The Welsh National costume has many variations but black and red are often the dominant colours. The dress can be made of black and white (or grey and white) Welsh cloth, with Mrs Moppety's bodice and sleeves, but a shorter skirt like the peasant. The apron is short and rounded and trimmed with lace. She is wearing a red flannel petticoat which shows below the skirt—alternatively this could be a strip of red flannel sewn to the hem of the skirt. The hat is made of thick black felt (flooring felt) or ordinary felt stiffened on the inside. The diameter of the brim is about 6 in., the side about 4 in. high. For details of how to make this hat see page 15. The underside of the brim is trimmed with white lace (or white felt cut with pinking scissors) and the hat tied to the head with black ribbons.

Harlequin: Make basic body as for the jester, using pink for the head and a lozenge-patterned fabric for the body. This fabric must be strong enough to take the strain of stuffing. The tunic can be adapted from the jester's by drawing a lengthened version of the front top section, placing the centre on the fold of double-thickness fabric and cutting out allowing $\frac{1}{3}$ in. seams. For the back, use the same pattern, but instead of placing pattern on fold cut out two pieces with seam allowance at centre back—this is to provide for a back opening. Armholes, neck and hem can be neatened with bias-binding for strength. Sew on a wide strip of black felt for belt and a yellow or white buckle at front (see pirate glove puppet, page 72). The mask and hat can also be made of black felt. The hat is made in the same way as the pirate's but using black thread for sewing. Sew the hat to the head to prevent it falling off. Make a white ruff like that for the clown in chapter 4 (page 19), but from 3 or 4 circles instead of one—cutting through each one once and sewing the cut edge to the next circle. When gathered up tightly to fit neck, this makes a much denser ruff.

Fig 79

Fig 80

Fig 81

Fig 82

7 Pivot-joint dolls

The pivot-joint doll is altogether more sophisticated in construction than the dolls in the previous chapters. The arms and legs can be moved round parallel to the sides of the body and—if sewn tightly enough—should stay in position, in the same way as many commercially made dolls or a teddy bear.

The head and the body are made of four pieces each, making the doll rounder and more shapely than, say, the single-hinged doll. The arms and legs are sewn to the body with button thread, using a button sewn to the inner side of each limb as an anchor. The three Victorian dolls wear variations of the same dress (Alice also has a bonnet and an apron) and they have the same looped fringe and pony tail. Features are a combination of felt and embroidery. The Indian woman is wearing a sari, which has been slightly adapted to make it easier for a child to take off and put on, and without having to re-pleat it each time.

Basic doll (about 17 in. high)

Materials
$\frac{1}{2}$ yd flesh-coloured cotton poplin, rayon, calico or similar fabric; 1 lb kapok; four buttons (about $\frac{3}{4}$ in. in diameter and with four sewing holes); long needle— 3–4 in. if possible; strong button thread; beeswax (optional).

To make
Draw pattern pieces (pattern no. 10) on to 1-in. squared paper and cut out. Place on double thickness fabric and draw round. Cut out, leaving $\frac{1}{3}$-in. seam allowance. With right sides facing, join head pieces at centre front and back, and body pieces at centre front and back. With right sides facing, join front head to front body across neck, back head to back body at neck (fig. 80). Trim sewn seams and—again with right sides facing—join front head and body to back head and body, leaving base open for stuffing. Trim seams and turn right side out. Stuff head and body firmly. Turn in seams at base and sew up opening.

With right sides facing, sew arms and legs, leaving tops open. Trim seams, particularly round thumbs and toes, and turn right side out. Using button thread, sew one button to the inside of each arm and leg, on the side nearest the body as marked on pattern, checking that the limbs will face front when sewn on. The sewn thread should show clearly as a cross on the right side of the fabric (fig. 81). Stuff arms and legs firmly, starting with the thumbs and toes. Turn in top seams and sew up openings. Using double thickness button thread and long needle, sew arms to body as follows: stitch first through the cross made by sewing on the button (i.e. not through fabric), then through the body, pulling tight, then through the cross on the other arm and back through the body again (fig. 82). Repeat this several times, pulling tight each time, then fasten off. The tighter the thread is pulled, the greater the friction and the better the arms will pivot. If the thread is too loose, the arms won't stay in a horizontal position but will tend to fall back to the vertical. Repeat this process for sewing on the legs. To make the button thread stronger, rub it with beeswax (or possibly candlewax) before sewing the limbs to the body. (Do this after threading needle.)

31

Emma

Materials

Body as basic doll; $1\frac{1}{2}$ oz dark yellow or light brown triple-knitting wool (yarn); $\frac{1}{2}$ yd light brown woven check cotton, or similar fabric; $\frac{1}{2}$ yd white lightweight cotton, lawn or similar fabric; $1\frac{3}{4}$–2 yds beige or white lace, about 2 in. wide; 1 yd white broderie anglaise or lace trimming; 1 yd narrow dark brown velvet ribbon; one mother-of-pearl button; shirring elastic; piece of light brown felt for shoes, white for buckle; scraps of blue and white felt for eyes, embroidery thread for features.

To make

Body: Make as basic doll.

Hair: Cut 46 lengths of wool, 20 in. long. Sew across centre. Lay across head and, starting slightly in front of seam, sew to head down centre parting. Arrange evenly round head and stitch wool to head at ear level. Wind 18 full turns of wool round a 13-in. piece of card. Remove from card and sew across 3 in. from one end. Using this 3 in. as fringe (bangs), place on head at right angles to first wool and sew to head, making sure the fringe is the correct length at front. Cut through loops at back, but leave for fringe. (See page 11 for diagram.) Tie brown velvet ribbon in bow round second lot of wool to make pony tail.

Features: Cut two circles out of blue felt and two ovals out of white felt for eyes. Glue or sew to face. Using a single strand of black embroidery thread, embroider a line of chain stitches all round each eye and single radiating stitches for eyelashes. Embroider two french knots in black for nose, two pink eight-point stars for cheeks and a red mouth in satin-stitch. (For embroidery stitches, see Features, page 13.)

Draw pattern pieces (pattern no. 10) on to 1-in. squared paper. Cut out and draw round on to appropriate fabrics. Cut out, allowing $\frac{1}{3}$-in. seams except where otherwise indicated. (For petticoat see pattern no. 11.)

Dress: With right sides facing, join side and shoulder seams, and back centre seam leaving top open. Sew a line of gathering stitches along the top of each sleeve as marked. With right sides facing, sew underarm seams. Pull gathering thread until sleeve opening corresponds to armhole opening, and knot. With right sides facing, pin sleeves to armholes, then sew together. Trim and/or neaten seams. Turn right side out. Sew a line of gathering stitches with shirring elastic round each sleeve as marked on pattern, pull to gather and fasten. Turn in sleeves at edge and hem (fig. 83). Sew two rows of wide beige or white lace round skirt of dress. Make jabot with two equal pieces of the same lace, about 4 in. long. Gather each piece at the top, sew one to the dress at neck, the second to the underside of the first about halfway down (fig. 84). Neaten cut sides if these are likely to fray. Sew brown velvet ribbon round neck opening instead of collar, covering top edge of jabot at front. Sew button to front centre of collar with brown thread.

Fig 83

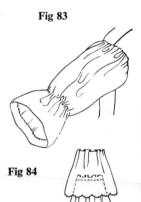

Fig 84

Petticoat: Using white fabric, make petticoat as for dress but without sleeves. Neaten armholes and neck. Check that hem is slightly shorter than dress and sew white broderie anglaise or lace to it. Sew snap fastener to back opening.

Pants: Using white fabric as for petticoat, these can be made short as for mother or daughter in chapter 5, or long as for Alice (page 65).

Shoes: Cut out shoes from brown felt. With right sides facing sew pairs together. Trim and turn right side out. Cut two circular buckles out of white felt and glue or sew to front.

Sock dolls (chapter 3)

Jack and Jill—one-pattern dolls (chapter 4)

Guardsman—one-pattern doll (chapter 4) 35

Father and mother, front and back views. Single-hinge doll family (chapter 5)

Opposite

Baby—single-hinge doll family (chapter 5)

Father—single-hinge doll family (chapter 5)

Single-hinge family, one-pattern dolls, and small sock doll

Son and daughter, front and back views. Single-hinge doll family (chapter 5) 41

Peasant girl with clothes. Double-hinge doll (chapter 6)

Peasant girl—double-hinge doll (chapter 6)

Mrs Moppety—double-hinge doll (chapter 6)   45

Jester—double-hinge doll (chapter 6)

Double-hinge dolls

Pivot-joint dolls

Alice and Indian girl—
pivot-joint dolls (chapter 7)

Two-headed doll—white girl (chapter 8)

Two-headed doll—black girl (chapter 8)

Red Indian glove puppet (chapter 9)

Clown glove puppet (chapter 9)

Pirate glove puppet (chapter 9)

Punch glove puppet with pattern pieces (chapter 9)

Glove and finger puppets
58

Punch and Judy with baby—glove puppets (chapter 9)

Finger puppets (chapter 10)

Victorian miniature dolls (chapter 11)

Butcher—miniature doll (chapter 11)

Louise

Materials

Body as basic doll (page 31); 1½ oz dark brown triple-knitting wool (yarn); 1 yd Regency stripe cotton in two shades of blue, or similar; white fabric and trimming as for Emma's underwear; 1 yd wide maroon or plum-coloured ribbon (velvet, silk or nylon); 1½ yds narrow matching velvet ribbon; snap fasteners; shirring elastic; piece of dark blue felt for shoes; blue and white felt and embroidery thread for features; 1 thick black or black and gold button and scraps of felt for cameo.

To make

Body: Make as basic doll.

Hair: Using dark brown wool, make as for Emma (page 32). Use narrow maroon or plum-coloured ribbon for bow.

Features: Make and embroider as for Emma.

Draw pattern pieces (pattern no. 10) on to 1-in. squared paper. Cut out and draw round on to appropriate fabrics. Cut out, allowing ⅓-in. seams except where otherwise indicated.

Dress: Using striped fabric, make dress as for Emma. When cutting out, the pattern can be laid on straight of fabric so that stripes run vertically on dress and horizontally on sleeves. Instead of ribbon at neck, neaten neckline. Frill: cut a length (or two lengths joined together) 48 in. long by 2⅔ in. wide, with the stripe running horizontally. Hem ⅓ in. at top and bottom—leaving a strip 2 in. wide. Pleat strip (fig. 85) and pin to skirt above hem. Adjust pleats if necessary so length of pleated strip equals width of skirt hem. Sew together and remove pins. Sew snap fasteners to back opening. Tie wide maroon or plum ribbon round waist with bow at the back.

Cameo: Sew button to the middle of a length of narrow maroon or plum ribbon. Glue a circle of turquoise or other felt to button, smaller than the button itself. On to this circle glue a smaller head-shaped piece of white felt. Tie ribbon tightly round doll's neck.

Underwear: Make from white fabric and trimming as for Emma.

Shoes: Using dark blue felt, cut out and make as above. Cut two 1-in. lengths of narrow velvet ribbon, turn in cut ends and glue to tops of shoes.

Fig 85

Alice

Materials

Body as basic doll (page 31); 1½ oz of dark brown triple-knitting wool (yarn); 1 yd pink Swiss cotton, or similar fabric with a self-colour pattern, or plain; ½ yd white cotton, cotton poplin or cotton/polyester mixture; 1½ yds white broderie anglaise or lace trimming; shirring elastic; narrow ordinary elastic; snap fasteners; piece of fine buckram or canvas; pink petersham ribbon; 1 yd narrow pink ribbon to match bonnet fabric; brown and white felt and embroidery thread for features; black felt for shoes, white for buckle.

To make

Body: Make as basic doll.

Hair: Using dark brown wool, make as for Emma, without ribbon.

Features: Make and embroider as for Emma, using brown felt for eyes.

Draw pattern pieces (pattern nos. 10 and 11) on to 1-in. squared paper. Cut out; draw round on to appropriate fabrics. Cut out, allowing ⅓-in. seams except

where otherwise indicated. When cutting out bonnet, cut either 2 of each pattern piece in the pink fabric or—if the fabric is very thin—1 of each plus one in a thicker fabric such as unbleached calico.

Dress: Using pink fabric, make as for Louise, including pleated frill, and with a plain neck and no sash.

Pants: With right sides facing, join seams at centre front and back. Trim and press seams open. With right sides facing join inside leg seam. Turn in waist hem, wide enough to allow for narrow elastic and leaving a small opening. Insert elastic through this opening. Turn right side out. Sew broderie anglaise or lace round leg openings (fig. 86). Neaten seams.

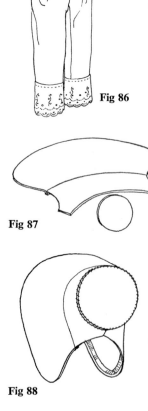

Fig 86

Fig 87

Fig 88

Apron: With right sides facing, join side and shoulder seams. Neaten these seams. Turn in and sew back openings, round neck, armholes and skirt hem. Sew broderie anglaise or lace trimming round armholes and skirt hem. Sew on one snap fastener at back neck.

Bonnet: With right sides facing, sew together the two brim pieces round the edge —i.e. either both of the same material, or one of some stiffer material (see cutting instructions above)—leaving the side AA open. Trim seams and turn right side out. With right sides facing, sew together the two side pieces round the edge, leaving the side BB open. Trim seams and turn right side out. With right sides facing (in this case the outside of the bonnet), sew AA to BB (fig. 87). Press open and neaten this seam. With right sides facing sew the two circular crown pieces together leaving an opening. Trim seam and turn right side out. Turn in seam at opening and sew up. Cut a circle out of buckram or canvas to match the crown and sew to the crown piece on the side which will be inside the bonnet. Pin CC to circular crown so that C1 just overlaps C2. Oversew together and join CD1 to CD2 on inside (fig. 88). At this stage petersham ribbon can be sewn all round inside edge of bonnet to stiffen it. Sew pink ribbons about 12 in. long to inside of bonnet on either side as marked on the pattern. Ribbon can be sewn to the outside of the bonnet to cover the joint. Put bonnet on head and tie under chin.

Shoes: Using black felt, make as for dolls above. Cut two square buckles out of white felt and glue to top.

Indian doll

Materials
Body as basic doll (page 31), using $\frac{1}{2}$ yd light brown cotton poplin or similar fabric; 1 oz black double-knitting, Courtelle or crepe wool (yarn), preferably slightly shiny; $\frac{3}{4}$ yd of 36-in. patterned sari fabric (silk, Madras cotton, chiffon or other lightweight fabric); $\frac{1}{4}$ yd plain coloured cotton or cotton poplin; snap fasteners; dark brown, pink and white felt scraps and embroidery thread for features.

To make
Body: Make as basic doll, using light brown fabric.

Hair: Cut 60 to 70 lengths of black wool, 22 in. long. Sew across centre. Place horizontally on head, and sew to head down centre parting. Make two plaits (braids) and fasten ends by winding round with black thread, then stitching through several times. Stitch to head at ear level. Trim ends.

Blouse: This short blouse, or Choli, is worn under the sari; here it is made of plain-coloured fabric, but it can be of the same fabric as the sari. Draw pattern piece (pattern no. 11) on to 1-in. squared paper and cut out. Place on double thickness fabric and draw round. Cut out (2 plus 2 for lining) allowing $\frac{1}{4}$-in.

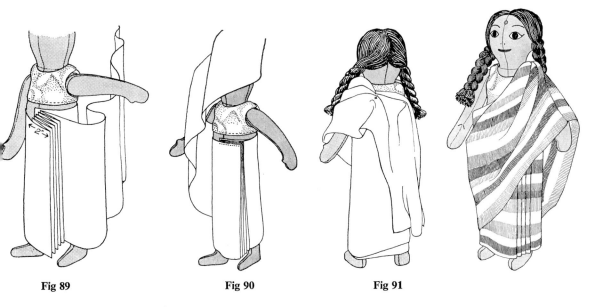

Fig 89   Fig 90   Fig 91

seams. With right sides facing, sew front to front lining from underarm A, round armhole, shoulder, neck, other shoulder and armhole, to other underarm A (see fig. 43, page 17). Trim seams to $\frac{1}{8}$ in. and turn right sides out. Press. Repeat for back and back lining. With front and back blouse facing, sew side seams AB together. Turn in edges BB and hem. Sew snap fasteners to shoulder openings.
Sari: Cut two strips of fabric approximately $9\frac{1}{2}$ in. by 36 in. (i.e. doll's waist to ankle measurement including seam allowance, by full width of fabric). Sew two strips together and hem raw edges all round. Alternatively this can be one continuous strip 2 yds long. Start by pinning sari to centre front waist. Wind round back of body from left to right, overlapping starting point. Make five knife pleats, each about 2 in. deep, and pin, then baste together (fig. 89). Make sure pleats fall straight and evenly. Wind round body again (fig. 90), then drape across chest from right to left and over left shoulder (fig. 91). If the sari drape is too long, you can adjust this either by making the pleats slightly wider, or by cutting off the surplus and re-hemming the raw edge. Sew snap fastener to first layer (the one first pinned to body) and to inner side of pleats—by fastening these two together the skirt will stay in position. Arrange draped sari in folds at back of shoulder and sew a snap fastener to the underside and to blouse (fig. 91).

Further suggestion

Pearly Queen: Make basic doll as above, with hairstyle like Mrs Moppety in chapter 6 (page 27). Make dress as for the Victorian girls in this chapter, out of black nylon velvet, with purple or black velvet ribbon cuffs instead of elasticized cuffs. Decorate dress with purple ribbon and patterns of pearl buttons, pearl sequins and pearl beads. Tie a small chiffon scarf round neck. The hat is made with a slightly curved brim and a low crown as in chapter 2, and decorated with a buckle and coloured feathers sewn over the crown. Shoes are made as for Louise (page 65).

8 Two-headed dolls

In the middle of the nineteenth century, doll manufacturers began to produce various kinds of mechanical and novelty dolls. Among these were dolls with two faces which, by the pulling of a cord (or a metal ring on the crown) could be made to smile on one side and cry on the other—the hair or bonnet concealing the second face. At about the same time dolls with two heads—one at either end of the body—also became popular. These had a wide skirt attached to the waist which served to hide whichever head was at the bottom. Occasionally this kind of doll can still be found: for instance I have one which was brought over from South America, and a few years ago an English manufacturer marketed a two-headed doll dressed in various ways—one was based on the rags to riches theme, another on the seasons of the year.

Here is a simple version of the two-headed doll with a black doll at one end and a contrasting white one at the other (also a popular Victorian motif). Like the double-jointed doll, each head is made of four pieces and each body of two. The arms are joined to the shoulders so that they swing up and down easily and don't stick out under the skirt. For the same reason the sleeves are short so as not to hinder the movement of the arms. The black doll has a bright-coloured patterned dress and white bias binding trim round collar and cuffs, the white doll has a light patterned dress and dark bias binding trim. The two skirts, which are very full and gathered, are sewn to the body at the waist and sewn together at the hem with white broderie anglaise or lace trimming between to give a neat finish. Obviously the clothes for this doll are not made to be taken off.

Black and white doll

Materials
$\frac{1}{4}$ yd unbleached calico or pink cotton; $\frac{1}{4}$ yd dark brown fabric of similar weight; $\frac{1}{2}$ yd each of contrasting fabrics: e.g. floral cottons, Vyella—not too stiff, otherwise the skirt won't fall easily; 1 yd white broderie anglaise or lace trimming for hem; white and dark-coloured bias bindings for collar and cuffs; $\frac{1}{2}$ oz yellow double-knitting wool (yarn); $\frac{1}{2}$ oz black double-knitting wool (yarn); scraps of felt for features; $\frac{3}{4}$–1 lb kapok.

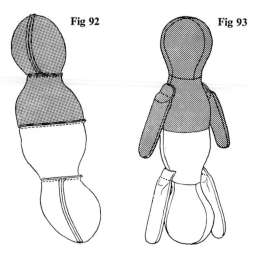

Fig 92   **Fig 93**

To make

Draw pattern pieces (pattern no. 12) on to 1-in. squared paper and cut out. Place on appropriate fabrics, double thickness where required, and draw round. Cut out, leaving $\frac{1}{4}$-in. seam allowance.

Body: With right sides facing sew front pink head pieces together at centre seam, and back pink head pieces at centre seam. Repeat for brown head. With right sides facing, sew front pink head to body across neck, and front brown head to body across neck. Repeat at back. With right sides facing, sew front pink and brown bodies together at waist (fig. 92), then back pink and brown bodies. Still with right sides facing, sew completed front to back, leaving opening as marked for stuffing. Trim all seams and turn right side out. Stuff firmly, particularly round necks, and sew up opening. With right sides facing, sew the arm pieces together to make four arms, leaving tops open for stuffing. Trim seams and turn right side out. Stuff firmly as far as dotted line, then sew a line of stitches across (seams at side). Turn top seams in and sew up openings. Sew arms to body, at shoulders (fig. 93): the arms should swing up and down easily.

Bodices: Make darts at front and back of each bodice. With right sides facing, join seams at sides and shoulders, leaving centre back open. Use bias binding to neaten neck and armholes, leaving half showing to make collar and cuffs (use white for black doll, dark for white doll—alternatively you could use lace or broderie anglaise trimming). Fit both bodices on doll. Turn in back openings and sew together. Stitch bodices to waist, turning seams under so that they meet in the centre.

Skirts: With right sides facing, join fronts to backs at side seams, leaving a slight opening at one side so that the skirts can be put on easily. Using two lines of stitching, gather each skirt at waist to match bodice (fig. 72, page 27). With right sides facing, sew waistbands to skirt waists (fig. 94). Turn open side of waistbands in and pin to doll, so that the two skirts touch. Sew waistbands to doll and sew up seam openings. Check skirt lengths, turn in hem of each and baste separately. Place broderie anglaise trimming between the two skirt hems and sew them together (fig. 95).

Hair: Using yellow wool, cut about 64 lengths, 15 in. long. Sew across middle, then sew to head down centre parting. Plait (braid) wool on either side of face and fasten by winding matching thread round ends, then stitching through several times. Trim ends. Catch stitch to head at ear level to keep in place. Repeat for black wool. (For diagrams, see page 11.)

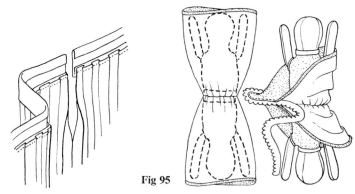

Fig 94   **Fig 95**

Features: Cut out two brown and two blue circles and four white ovals for eyes, pink circles for noses, red crescents for mouths. Glue or sew on faces.

N.B. When making doll check that both ends face in the same direction and that bodice openings really are at the back.

Further suggestions

Cinderella: Make body as above using pink fabric for both ends. Before the arrival of the fairy godmother, Cinderella wears a plain brown or grey dress which could have patches or darns sewn to it. Her hair is made as above, either plaited (braided) or in bunches. After the transformation, she wears a white or pale-coloured satin dress with a blue ribbon sash across one shoulder decorated with a silver (or white) and blue star, and lace round collar, cuffs and decorating the skirt. Her hair can be made in the same way as that for the mother in chapter 5 or Mrs Moppety in chapter 6, but using less wool. The headband or tiara could be silver ribbon or trimming or even tinsel.

Night and day: This doll is awake at one end and asleep at the other. Again the body is made as above using pink fabric at both ends. Awake, she has a dress made as for the black and white doll from brightly coloured fabric. Her hair is also made as above but with the addition of a fringe (bangs) (see Hair, chapter 2) and short bunches instead of plaits (braids). Asleep, she wears a nightdress of plain white, pink or light blue with a frilly trim down centre front and around armholes (frill trimming with ribbon threaded down the centre can be bought by the yard). The mob cap is made of the same material as the nightdress and in the same way as for Mrs Moppety in chapter 6, but smaller and with only a narrow width between the outer edge and gathering: tie it under the chin with narrow ribbon. Nose and mouth are the same both ends. The eyes are made of felt circles at the awake end, and embroidered eyelashes sewn with black embroidery thread at the asleep end.

9 Glove puppets

Glove puppets are popular with children of all ages. Babies love to watch them, pre-school children act out their fantasies through them and older children use them to give puppet theatre performances. Once you have a basic pattern to work from, any number of different characters can easily be made.

These puppets are made of felt (except for the hair), which comes in a great many bright colours and is easy to work with because the edges don't fray and can be left raw. They are made basically on one principle: the front and back are prefabricated separately before being sewn together, the head is stuffed and has a piece of cardboard roll in the neck to stiffen it. The Indian, clown and pirate have round faces with side seams, but the Punch and Judy have their head seam from front to back so that the nose and chin—an essential feature—can be the correct shape.

It is important not to stuff the head too full, so that there is plenty of room for a finger, otherwise it is difficult to manipulate. Before using these patterns check that they fit the size of hand they will be used for, although they have been designed to fit a medium-sized child's or small adult's hand and should be correct in most cases. For very young children it is probably better to sew on the features as these tend to get pulled off; but if glue is used it should be applied very sparingly, otherwise it tends to soak through the felt and look messy.

If the puppets are being sewn by machine, white cotton can be used throughout as the white stitching accentuates the various trimmings and gives the puppets a professional look. Raw edges should be cut very neatly where left open and a really sharp pair of scissors is essential for this purpose. The puppets are approximately 11–12 in. high.

Red Indian

Materials

¼ yd or two 9-in. squares of orange felt for dress, pieces of light brown felt for head and hands, dark brown and kingfisher blue for dress trimmings, scraps for features; black double-knitting wool (yarn) for hair; 1½-in. length of cardboard roll 1 in. in diameter (this can be made by gluing together the ends of a piece of 1½-in.-wide card); a feather; kapok.

To make

Draw pattern pieces (pattern no. 13) on to 1-in. squared paper and cut out. Draw round on to appropriate coloured felts, allowing seams only where indicated.
Head: With right sides facing join pieces leaving neck open, trim and turn right side out. Stuff (not neck) with kapok. Insert cardboard roll and glue or sew to felt. A circle of felt glued to top of cardboard roll before inserting in neck will stop the kapok coming out (fig. 96).
Body: Sew front hands and cuffs to front body, and back hands and cuffs to back, with a line of stitching through the three layers (fig. 97). Sew blue and brown felt neck trimming to front with a double line of stitching, and front and back hem trimming with a single line of stitching as marked on pattern (fig. 98). With right sides facing, join front and back body pieces leaving hem and neck open and making sure brown collar is left loose and not sewn into seam by mistake. Trim seams particularly round hands, under arms and at shoulders. Turn right side out. Insert neck into body and sew or glue together. Join brown collar

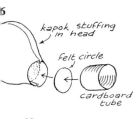

kapok stuffing in head

felt circle

cardboard tube

cuff

body

Fig 97

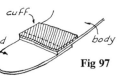

Fig 98

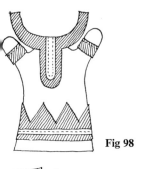

Fig 99

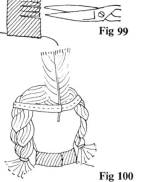

Fig 100

71

pieces at back. With sharp pair of scissors cut cuffs into fringes (fig. 99) and—optional—trim hem with pinking shears.

Hair: Cut wool (yarn) into 35 lengths, 15 in. long. Sew to head at centre parting (see chapter 2). Plait (braid) it on either side of head and fasten ends by winding round several times with black thread, then stitching through wool. Stitch hair to head at ear level on either side to hold in place. Sew on head band, inserting feather at back (fig. 100).

Features: Cut out and glue or sew features to face, using black circles on white ovals for eyes, brown triangle for nose and pink or red for mouth.

Clown

Materials

One 9-in. square each of turquoise and green felt, pieces of white for head, hands and buttons, kingfisher blue for collar and cuffs, scraps for features. Orange double-knitting wool (yarn) for hair, a length of black wool for eyes. Cardboard roll and kapok as above. Alternative suggestions for dress colours: dark orange and brown with light orange collar and cuffs, purple and red with mauve.

To make

Draw pattern pieces (pattern no. 13) and cut out as for Indian.

Head: Make as for Indian.

Body: Overlap left-hand pieces on to right-hand and sew centres (fig. 101). Sew hands and cuffs to front and back body (as for Indian) and with right sides facing join front to back as above. Insert neck into body and sew or glue together. Sew collar to neck, joining at back. Glue on felt buttons. (If you have no pinking shears, plain circles look just as effective.)

Fig 101

Hair: Wind orange wool round a piece of card approximately $3\frac{1}{2}$ in. $\times$ $4\frac{1}{2}$ in. long. Remove from card and machine or sew through centre (fig. 102). Pin to head with seam running horizontally from side seam across back to opposite side seam at about eye level. Sew to head along seam in wool (fig. 103). Cut through loops, and trim.

Features: With black wool sew two large crosses for eyes. Glue or sew dark pink or red circle for nose, wide red crescent for mouth, and black eyebrows.

Fig 102

Pirate

Materials

$\frac{1}{4}$ yd or two 9-in. squares of blue felt; a 12-in. or similar piece of red felt for scarf and vest stripes; pink felt for face and hands, black felt for hat, belt, beard and eye-patch, yellow for buckle, white for vest and skull and crossbones, scraps for eye, nose and mouth; cardboard roll and kapok as for Indian (page 71); brass curtain ring.

To make

Draw pattern pieces (pattern no. 14) and cut out as above, cutting part of the way down centre front, as indicated on pattern.

Head: Make as for Indian, but pink.

Body: Sew hands to front and back body (as for Indian, but without cuffs). Sew black belt to front and to back, as indicated on pattern, with a line of stitching at top and bottom. Sew yellow buckle to front. Glue four strips of red to white vest. Turn back blue centre front flaps to make collar and sew or glue vest to it (fig. 104). With right sides facing sew front and back together. (This time the collar

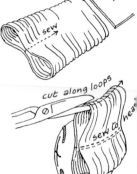

Fig 103

72

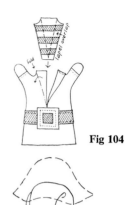

Fig 104

Fig 105

should be sewn into seam. You may need to pin lapel back until this is done.) Trim and turn right side out. Insert neck and sew or glue together.

Scarf: Pin centre of longest side of red triangle to top of head, slightly over seam. Take sides back to nape, fold over neatly and pin to head; now bring the top of the triangle down, so that all three corners meet, tucking the sides in underneath (fig. 105). Sew together at nape and at strategic places to hold to head.

Hat: On right side of felt sew hat pieces together with white machine-stitching, leaving head opening. Put on to head and sew to head through scarf. Glue on skull and crossbones.

Features: Glue or sew eye (blue circle on white oval), eyebrow, triangular nose, mouth, and beard and eyepatch (as pattern)—tucking the ends of the eyepatch under scarf. Sew curtain ring at ear level on opposite side to eyepatch.

Punch and Judy

Materials

$\frac{1}{4}$ yd purple and $\frac{1}{4}$ yd red felt; pink felt for face and hands; pieces of yellow for Punch's collar and hatband and Judy's buttons; black for buckle, white for Judy's cap, apron and cuffs and Punch's buttons; scraps for features; brown double-knitting wool (yarn) for Judy's hair; cardboard roll and kapok as for Indian (page 71). Punch's hat is red one side, purple the other. Both Punch and Judy have purple front bodies and red backs.

To make Punch

Draw pattern pieces (pattern no. 13) and cut out as for Indian.

Head: Sew purple and red hat pieces to face pieces at dotted line (fig. 106). With right sides facing, sew head together. Trim carefully at nose, chin and hat point. Turn right side out, stuff, and insert cardboard roll as described on page 71. Make sure nose and chin are well stuffed.

Body: Sew hands and belt to body as for pirate, using purple body and red belt at front, red body and purple belt at back. Sew on black buckle. With right sides facing, sew front to back, trim and turn right side out. Insert neck into body and glue or sew together. Sew on yellow hatband and collar with joins at back.

Features: Glue or sew on buttons, eyes (blue circles on white ovals), black eyebrows and red mouth.

To make Judy

Draw pattern pieces (pattern nos 13 and 14) and cut out as above. The edges of the apron and cap brim can be plain or pinked.

Head: Sew the two pieces together leaving neck open, trim carefully and proceed as above.

Body: Sew hands and cuffs to body, sew front to back and join head to body, all as above.

Apron: Stitch apron to strip and sew to dress, joining at back.

Hair: Wind 15 full winds round a 16-in.-wide piece of card. Remove from card and sew through middle to head at centre parting. Take hair on both sides of face round to back, twist into bun shape (fig. 107). Sew through wool so bun stays in place, and sew to head above nape of neck.

Cap: Sew loose line of stitching round outer rim of crown (fig. 108); draw thread so circumference matches inner circle of brim (fig. 109). Pin and sew inner brim and crown together on underside (fig. 110); sew to head so that hair shows.

Features: Glue or sew on eyes (brown circles on white ovals), brown eyebrows and mouth.

Fig 106

Fig 107

Baby

Materials

Pink felt for body; white felt for swaddling clothes; scraps for features; blue, pink or yellow ribbon; kapok.

To make

Draw pattern pieces (pattern no. 14) and cut out as above—the swaddling clothes are made of three identical pieces using the pattern for Judy's apron.

Body: With right sides facing, sew together leaving opening for stuffing. Trim and turn right side out. Stuff well. Sew up opening.

Clothes: With curved edge at top, arrange one apron shape around baby's head, stitching to body at middle and with two tucks at forehead (fig. 111). Sew other two apron shapes together on right side, leaving straight side open. Slip baby into the pocket thus made and stitch to body and 'head shawl'.

Features: Glue on blue circles for eyes, pink circle for nose and red for mouth. Tie ribbon round middle, fastening to body with a few stitches.

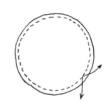

Fig 108

Fig 109

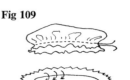

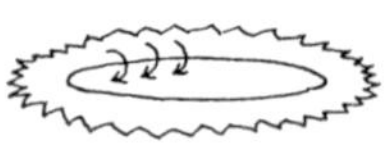

Fig 110

Further suggestions

Father Christmas: Use basic head and dress pattern (as Indian, page 71) with pink felt for head and hands, red for body, white for cuffs and trimmings. The hood is made with two pieces of red felt sewn together at top and back, with a white strip sewn around face opening, and turned under and sewn to body at neck. Hair can be white wool (yarn) loops sewn round top of head from ear to ear. Beard can be made like pirate's (page 73) or with white wool wound round three fingers, fastened together at one end and sewn to face, using short lengths of wool knotted in the middle for a moustache.

Witch: Make as for Indian—or as Judy (page 73) for more pronounced features —using dark green for dress, with yellow random stars and moon glued or sewn to it, black for hat, green or white wool for hair. The hair is made as for Indian but left loose and stitched to head at ears to keep in place. The hat is made as shown in chapter 2. She could also have a simple black cloak. A wizard could be made in the same way using black or purple for body and hat, white for hair (shorter than witch).

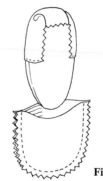

Fig 111

74

King: Use purple for dress trimmed with gold braid and a hem of white fleur-de-lys. The crown is made with a circle of purple felt gathered as Judy's cap—but smaller—with a white band for brim and gold braid trim (see fig. 113, page 77). A piece of red felt with white edging does for a cloak and black wool stitching along the white edging of cloak and crown give an ermine effect. A queen can be made in the same way.

Monk: Use brown felt, with circular collar with front opening and braid for belt. The hair can be stitched in short loops all the way round or made as for the clown (page 72), using twice the length, less width and much less wool—so that it falls in a downward direction.

Ringmaster: Use red for body with black felt bow tie and yellow buttons. Collar, cuffs and pockets add interest. Top hat is made as in chapter 2, using black flooring felt, or ordinary felt stiffened on the inside with card, buckram or canvas.

Mandarin: Yellow head and hands, turquoise, blue, green or other colour for body. Add different coloured strips round hem and long strips at wrists for deep cuffs—these should be sewn on *after* assembly. The pigtail can be made of felt, or plaited (braided) black wool sewn to back of head.

10   Finger puppets

When our young son was in hospital with his leg in traction, my husband drew funny faces on his toenails to amuse him. Similarly, at school we used to draw faces on our fingernails and wiggle them at each other in class. We also knotted handkerchiefs to make rabbits or people. Finger puppets are the natural outcome of such simple amusements. They are particularly good playthings for children who are ill and have to spend long periods in bed amusing themselves. As with the glove puppets, once you have a basic pattern, any number of characters can be made quite simply—characters from nursery rhymes or stories, Little Red Riding Hood and the wolf, witches and fairies, cowboys and Indians, or just everyday people like a policeman, a teacher, the milkman or a family.

When you are making something as small as this it is very important to keep everything very simple and to avoid too many fiddly bits of sewing, or fraying edges. Felt is very useful here, both for head and hands and also for the main body when this is to be in a plain colour. Lace edging, braid, ribbon, etc., are easier to trim with than trying to cut up small pieces of fabric which need sewn hems.

The general effect is more important than accurate detail and sometimes just one feature and the right colours are enough to make the character recognizable.

These finger puppets are made very much like the glove puppets, but without a cardboard roll in the neck and with a single thickness of felt for the hands. With the exception of the Scotsman they can all be made using the following basic pattern. The measurements are approximate only, as the size of the puppet depends on the size of the finger for which it is intended.

Basic pattern (about 4 in. high)

Materials
Piece of pink or other flesh-coloured felt about 3–4 in. square; kapok or cotton-wool (absorbent cotton); piece of felt or fabric about 6 in. × 3 in.

To make
Draw head, body and hand shapes on to paper as fig. 112. The approximate measurements given are to the sewing line (dotted).

Fig 112

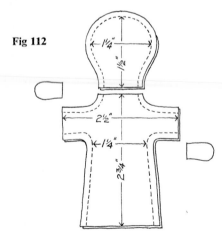

Fig 113

Head: Draw round head shape on double thickness pink felt and cut out allowing seams as shown. With right sides facing sew together as dotted line leaving neck open. Trim seam if necessary and turn right side out. Stuff with kapok or cotton-wool (absorbent cotton) leaving neck free. Glue a small piece of felt to the kapok by inserting it through the neck opening, to prevent the stuffing escaping.

Body: Draw round body pattern on to double thickness felt or fabric and cut out allowing seams as shown—if using fabric allow seams also at hem, wrists and neck. With right sides facing, sew sides and shoulders together. Trim seams carefully and turn right side out. Cut out the two hands from pink felt, insert one in each sleeve and sew across. Insert head in neck opening and sew to body all round. If using fabric for body, turn in seams at wrists when sewing in hands, at neck when sewing in head, and at hem.

King

Materials

Pieces of pink, purple and white felt; black 3-ply, 4-ply or double-knitting wool (yarn); gold braid; 2 small silvered, white or mother-of-pearl buttons with concealed holes; embroidery (or ordinary) cotton thread; kapok or cotton-wool (absorbent cotton).

To make

Draw patterns and make head and body as basic puppet, using purple for body. With black wool sew hair in loops as for sock doll, chapter 3. Embroider features using brown or black for eyes and eyebrows, pink for nose and red for mouth. Sew a length of gold braid down the front of the body.

Cape: Cut out a circle of white felt, $2\frac{3}{4}$ in. diameter. Cut away a one-third segment and cut out an inner circle to fit the king's neck. Sew running stitches in black round the edges to look like ermine. Fasten cape at front by sewing to neck with a button.

Crown: Cut a circle, about $2\frac{1}{4}$ in. in diameter, out of purple felt. Sew a line of gathering stitches round the edge, pull together until the opening fits the top of the king's head (fig. 113) and fasten. Sew two pieces of gold braid over the top of the crown at right angles. Cut a strip of white felt the same length as the crown's circumference and again sew a line of running stitches along the centre with black wool (fig. 113). Sew to crown, then sew to head. Now sew one button to the centre where the gold braid crosses and, before fastening off, a couple of stitches through to the head to pull the centre of the crown in slightly.

Princess

Materials

Pink felt; floral cotton or similar fabric; yellow wool (yarn); small piece of white trimming; small length of gold rick-rack braid; embroidery thread; kapok or cotton-wool (absorbent cotton).

To make

Draw patterns and make head and body as basic puppet, remembering to leave seam allowances at base, wrists and neck. Embroider eyes in blue, nose in pink and mouth in red. Cut eight short lengths of yellow wool (yarn) and sew to top of head as fringe (bangs). Wind 12 full winds of yellow wool (more if 3 ply) round a piece of card 4¼ in. long, remove from card, lay across head over fringe and sew to head at centre parting. Catch stitch to head all round at ear level. Sew a circle of gold rick-rack braid to top of head to form a small crown. Sew white trimming to neck at front: the one in the illustration is one segment of a flower-like trimming, but you could use lace round the neck or down the front.

Queen

Materials
Pink, red and white felt; brown wool (yarn); length of black wool (yarn); embroidery thread; gold braid; small button; kapok or cotton-wool (absorbent cotton).

To make
Draw patterns and make head and body as basic puppet using red for dress and crown. Leaving out the fringe (bangs), make hair as for Princess, but slightly longer. Twist ends and sew into a bun at back of head. Embroider features using brown for eyes, pink for nose, red for mouth. Make crown as for king, but smaller and without button. Sew to head. Sew a length of gold braid down front of body. Cut a strip of white felt for collar, sew running stitches with black wool and fasten at neck by sewing on button. The button in the illustration has been decorated with felt pens.

Witch

Materials
White, dark green and black felt; light green wool (yarn); embroidery thread; kapok or cotton-wool (absorbent cotton).

To make
Draw patterns and make head and body as basic puppet, using white for head and hands, green for body. Make hair as for princess, without fringe (bangs). Cut loops. Embroider face, using green for eyes, nose and eyebrows, red for mouth. Make hat from a cone and circular brim as described in chapter 2.

Fairy

Materials
Pink felt; white felt or cotton fabric; white or silver wool (yarn); about ½ yd lingerie edging or similar lacy frill; embroidery thread; kapok or cotton-wool (absorbent cotton); length of gold rick-rack or other braid; optional—light-weight cocktail stick (e.g. plastic) and small piece of gold paper for wand.

To make
Draw patterns and make head and body as basic puppet, using white for body. Sew hair in loops as for king (page 77). Embroider face, using blue for eyes, pink for nose, red for mouth. Sew gold braid round head at forehead. Wind frill round body three times in layers, starting near the hem and finishing at the waist, sewing it on as you go. Sew a second piece of frill round the neck as a cape, with opening at the front. Wand (optional): cut a star out of double thickness of gold paper and glue together with end of cocktail stick between. Sew other end of stick to right hand of fairy. The hand could be curled round the stick. It is important that the cocktail stick is light in weight otherwise it will pull the puppet over.

Mexican

Materials

Light brown, yellow and dark yellow or orange felt; brightly coloured striped fabric; embroidery thread; kapok or cotton-wool (absorbent cotton); red rick-rack braid.

To make

Draw patterns and make head and body as basic puppet, using light brown for head and hands, yellow for body. Embroider face, using black for eyes and eyebrows and moustache (sewn in long loops), medium brown for nose, red for mouth.

Poncho: Cut a lozenge-shape out of the striped material, so that the length equals nearly twice the length of the body (about 5 in.) and the width equals the shoulder width (about 2 in.) Allow for hem all round. Cut a slit across the middle to fit neck, and hem all raw edges. The slit need not be very big if the poncho is fitted on to the body before the head is inserted.

Hat: Using dark yellow or orange felt, make hat as for witch, but with the following differences (fig. 114): the cone should be rounded at the top, and the brim should be much wider than the witch's and have a V-shape cut out of it, so that when the two sides of the V are sewn together the brim curls upwards. Sew red rick-rack braid round underside of brim, and sew hat to head.

Japanese girl

Materials

White felt; patterned silk, cotton or similar fabric with an oriental look; ½ yd matching plain ribbon, ½ in. wide; black wool (yarn); embroidery thread; kapok or cotton-wool (absorbent cotton).

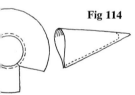

Fig 114

To make

Draw patterns and make head and body as basic puppet. Make hair as for princess, but slightly longer and cutting through the loops. Wind a length of black wool round your little finger, place on top of head and sew to head firmly making sure it cannot unravel. Cut a short length of ribbon (about 1½–2 in.), fold it in half and sew it tightly round the bun where it meets the head. Embroider eyes and eyebrows in black, mouth in red and small black stitches for nose. Place the rest of the ribbon round the neck of the puppet—as you would for tying a tie—cross the two ends over the chest, take them round to the back and tie into a bow. Stitch the bow to the dress at back to keep it in place. To make it more like a real Japanese costume, bring the two loops together in front of the knot and stitch the inner sides together (fig. 115). Pieces of split matchsticks (rubbed smooth on sandpaper) could be pushed through the top of the bun at right angles for decoration.

Fig 115

Arab

Materials

Medium brown and yellow or buff felt; white cotton fabric; two lengths of dark brown wool (yarn); embroidery thread; kapok or cotton-wool (absorbent cotton).

To make

Draw patterns and make head and body as basic puppet, using medium brown felt for head and hands and white cotton for body. Make sleeveless coat from a rectangular piece of yellow or buff felt 2¼ in. high by 3 in. wide, by cutting a slit in each side for the arms. Embroider eyes and eyebrows in black, nose in dark brown, mouth in red. Sew loops of dark brown wool for beard and moustache. *Head-dress:* This is a strip of cotton, hemmed all round, 7 in. long by 1¼ in. wide. Place it well forward across the head leaving equal lengths either side and pin in position. Pull the two edges together behind the head and flatten the resultant fold on top of them (fig. 116). Pin. Wind a length of brown wool round crown of head and sew this through the head-dress to the head. Remove pins. Join adjacent edges of strip down centre back to keep in place.

Fig 116

Scotsman

Materials

Pink and light grey felt; scraps of yellow, light brown and black felt; piece of tartan fabric approximately 12 in. × 2 in.; rust-red wool (yarn); embroidery thread; length of red wool (yarn); kapok or cotton-wool (absorbent cotton).

To make

Draw patterns for head and hands as basic puppet. Draw pattern for jacket as basic body but cut off at the waist—straight at back and with an inverted V at front. Proceed as for basic puppet, using light grey for jacket.

Kilt: Cut a piece of tartan fabric 7 in. × 2 in., and hem one side (if this is the selvedge, there is no need to hem and the material can measure 1¾ in. instead). Fold into pleats starting from centre front (fig. 117) pinning each pleat, until the kilt fits the waist of jacket. Stitch back seam together on inside. Stitch each pleat down to keep in place. Insert kilt into jacket opening and sew together. Cut out a round sporran shape in light brown felt and glue a small fringed strip of black felt to it. Sew sporran to kilt at waist.

Sew or glue a strip of black felt from back left waist across right shoulder to front left waist. Sew or glue a small yellow buckle to it at front. Embroider eyes in blue, nose in pink and mouth in red. With rust wool sew loops for hair (as for king) and for beard.

Plaid: From the remaining tartan, cut a right-angled triangle with a 2-in. base and a 4½-in. perpendicular and hem all round. Sew the base to jacket at back waist and the point to left shoulder at front (fig. 117).

Beret: Using light grey felt throughout make as for sailor (see Suggestions, page 25) with narrower band. Sew to head. Make pom-pom with red wool and sew through to head to keep beret flat on top.

Further suggestions

Red Indian chief: Make in felt as basic pattern, using brown for head and hands, orange for body. Cut a fringe round hem and add a fringed collar and decorations. The hair is made from black wool, the head-dress can be made from tiny chicken feathers or pieces of white felt dipped in black ink.

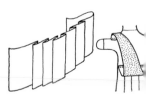

Fig 117

Policeman: Make in felt as basic pattern using navy blue for body. Add black belt and collar, white buckle and buttons, and give him a wool or felt moustache. The helmet is two pieces of navy felt sewn together on the wrong side with a white felt badge at front. Put a little stuffing in the helmet before sewing to head so that it keeps its shape.

80

Eastern prince: Make as for Arab using richer colours and without the head-dress. Add a ribbon sash. The turban is made by stitching a small shallow cup shape, like the crown of a hat, to the head; take a long length of white bias binding and starting at the middle of the head at the back, bring the two ends of the binding to the front, cross at the forehead and round to the back again. Repeat until only a little of the black felt shows. Stitch carefully so that overlap stays in place and finish off with a small circle of felt and fringed silver or gold paper.

Beefeater: Make of felt as basic pattern using red for body. Add strips of yellow felt and other decorations (the strips could be sewn on with black thread). The collar is made of two circles of white felt pinked round the outer edge and with a smaller circle cut out of the middle. It should be added before the head is sewn to the body. The hat, made as in chapter 2, can be of felt or black card, with red, white and blue felt or paper round the band.

Teacher: Make in felt as basic pattern, using grey for body. Before sewing to head, cut down centre front of body, turn back flaps and stick a white felt shirt front with black felt strip for tie to the underneath (see pirate in chapter 9). Add white felt collar. The gown is made as for the Arab. The mortar-board is made of a small square of black felt sewn to the head with a square of thin black card sewn to it through the centre; the tassel can be made from cotton or embroidery thread. The spectacles are two semicircles of white felt.

11 Miniature dolls

Dolls' houses have been popular since the seventeenth century and many beautiful examples—particularly German, Dutch and English ones—can be seen in collections today. They are of great interest to social historians because they give an accurate picture, down to the minutest detail, of contemporary home life. The dolls who lived in these fine mansions were often elaborately dressed in the latest fashions. They were made of wax, fabric, jointed wood and (in the nineteenth century) porcelain and bisque.

Victorian children also used to dress miniature dolls in characters from their favourite plays, and Queen Victoria as a child had a collection of little Dutch dolls which she dressed herself, and which are now part of the London Museum collection. Nowadays children, and adults, often collect small souvenir dolls dressed in national or historical costumes.

The miniature dolls here are made of pipe-cleaners, covered with kapok or cotton-wool (absorbent cotton) and then felt. One of the advantages of using pipe-cleaners is that the doll can be made to bend easily. Another is that the size of doll can be altered by a couple of extra twists where required.

Making the clothes for such small dolls can be an intricate business but, although you want to keep everything as simple as possible as with the finger puppets in the previous chapter, unlike the finger puppets, half the charm of these dolls is often in the accurate detailing. Lace, ribbon and other ready-made trimmings are again useful here; so is felt. It is best to keep fabric patterns in scale with the size of doll where possible. As the clothes are sewn to the doll, it is possible to cheat a little—for instance, a shirt under a jacket need not have sleeves; and once a dress is on a doll the opening can be sewn together. Minor mistakes in size can be rectified as you go along. But always check each garment piece against the doll before starting to sew.

Basic doll (height about 6 in.)

Materials
3 pipe-cleaners; kapok or cotton-wool (absorbent cotton); sewing thread; flesh-coloured felt; bias binding; soldering wire (optional).

To make
Take two pipe-cleaners, twist them round each other twice at the centre and bend two ends upwards, two ends down (fig. 118, left). Twist the upward ends round each other to form the trunk and head, leaving the downward ends as the legs. Bend the bottom of the legs at right angles to make feet. Take the third pipe-cleaner and twist it round the body a couple of times at shoulder height (fig. 118, right). If the arms are too long, bend the ends back towards the middle and twist them round. At this stage the whole doll can be altered to make it smaller, the legs can be twisted upwards in the same way as the arms, and the body twisted round several extra times above the leg join.

Wind kapok or cotton-wool (absorbent cotton) round arms, legs and trunk (and a little round head), enough to make a good-shaped body. Wind sewing thread round the kapok to hold it in place. Cut two head shapes out of felt as for the finger puppets in chapter 10 (page 76). With right sides facing, sew together leaving neck open. Trim and turn right side out. Put over pipe-cleaner head and stuff with kapok or cotton-wool with the aid of a knitting needle.

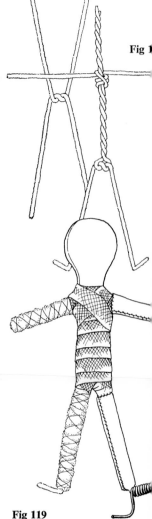

Fig 1

Fig 119

82

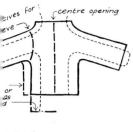

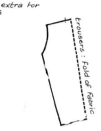

Fig 120

Cut rectangular pieces of felt equalling the length and circumference of the arms and legs. Place round each arm and leg and oversew under arms, across ends of hands and inside legs. Wind bias binding round trunk (fig. 119) and sew the ends to prevent them coming undone. Also sew felt arms, legs and head to the binding to stop them slipping off.

Soldering wire wound round each foot will weight the doll so that it will stand up on its own (fig. 119). In this case stop kapok at ankle, and when making shoes be sure the opening is large enough to go over the wire. Soldering wire is obtainable from ironmongers or hardware shops; it is very pliable and can be cut with scissors.

Victorian father

Materials
Body as basic doll; dark brown 3- or 4-ply wool (yarn); embroidery thread for features; white fabric for shirt; black or grey and white checked fabric for trousers; pieces of white, yellow and black felt; small length of black cord or narrow ribbon for bow tie.

To make
Body: Make as for basic doll.
Hair: With brown wool sew long stitches all round head from centre parting to sides and back (see chapter 2), then loops at front from ear to ear for sideboards and beard.
Features: Embroider eyes and eyebrows black, mouth red, and two french knots for nose.
Clothes: Lay doll on a sheet of paper and draw basic patterns (fig. 120). Make sure the widths are adequate, so that the sleeves, etc., won't be too tight. Remember to allow for seams where necessary when cutting out.
Shirt. Using the basic pattern, without sleeves, cut out shirt from white fabric with opening at the back. With right sides facing, sew front to back at sides and

shoulders. Trim, turn right side out and put on doll. Sew up back opening. Cut out a narrow strip of white felt for collar, slightly curved at the ends. Fit round neck, with opening at the front, and sew to shirt. Tie black cord round neck with knot at front and sew on firmly. *Trousers.* Using basic trouser pattern and checked fabric make trousers (as for instance Jack's trousers, but without straps, page 19). Put on doll and sew to waist. Turn in and hem trouser legs. *Waistcoat.* Cut out a rectangular piece of yellow felt, wide enough to reach from the doll's shoulder to below the waist and long enough to go round the waist plus an overlap. Cut two oval holes for arms and shape the waistcoat at front (fig. 121). Put on doll and sew together at front with two rows of black french knots for buttons. *Jacket.* Using black felt, cut out basic pattern to slightly below the waist with opening at front. With right sides facing sew front to back at shoulders, sides and sleeves. Trim and turn right side out. Cut out a rectangular piece of black felt about $1\frac{1}{2}$ in. wide and about $1\frac{1}{2}$ in. longer than the waist measurement of top jacket. Make a box pleat in the middle back with the extra $1\frac{1}{2}$ in. and sew to jacket all round (fig. 122). Turn lapels back at front and glue, or sew, to shoulders. *Shoes.* Draw pattern as fig. 123, to fit foot. Cut out two from black felt. Fold each piece in half and oversew at front and back, leaving a big enough opening to slip over foot. Put on foot and glue or sew to keep in place. Alternatively the back can be left open and glued together and to heel after slipping on foot.

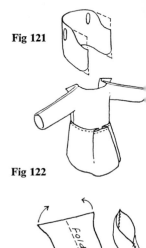

Fig 121

Fig 122

Fig 123

Mother

Materials
Body as basic doll; brown 3- or 4-ply wool (yarn); embroidery thread for features; plain coloured satin, small woven check cotton or other fabric; 1 yd narrow lace trimming; felt for shoes to match dress.

To make
Body: Make as basic doll, slightly smaller than father.
Hair: With brown wool, sew long stitches from centre parting to sides, then longish loops at ear level on either side of face. Bring needle out at centre top of head, loop wool round several times to make a small bun and sew firmly through loops all round and to head.
Features: Embroider as for father, using brown for eyes and eyebrows.
Clothes: Lay doll on a sheet of paper and draw basic pattern for bodice including sleeves (fig. 120). Make sure sleeve widths are adequate, but don't make waist much wider than the doll's. Cut out bodice with opening at the back. With right sides facing, sew front bodice to back at sides, shoulders and sleeves. Cut a rectangle of fabric for the skirt approximately 10 in. × 3 in. (length from waist to ankle). With right sides facing, sew skirt seam. Sew a line of gathering stitches round top of skirt and pull in until it matches the bodice, then sew skirt to bodice with seams at back. Trim all seams, turn right side out. Turn in neck, wrists and skirt hem and sew. Sew three rows of lace round skirt, the bottom one overlapping the hem. Put on doll. Sew up back bodice opening. Sew lace round wrists, and from centre back waist over shoulders to centre front to make a V-shape at front and back. *Shoes.* Make as for father.

Daughter

Materials
Body as basic doll, but using white felt for legs; yellow 3- or 4-ply wool (yarn); embroidery thread for features; plain coloured satin or striped cotton or other

fabric; short length of 2-in. white broderie anglaise trimming, or white cotton and narrow lace trimming, for pants; $\frac{1}{2}$ yd lace; $\frac{1}{4}$ yd narrow ribbon; black felt for shoes.

To make
Body: Make as basic doll but smaller, using pink felt for arms, white felt for legs to look like stockings.
Hair: Using yellow wool, sew several longish loops at top of head for fringe. Then sew long stitches round head from centre parting to sides and back (as for father). Sew long loops from ear to ear round back of head (see chapter 2).
Features: Embroider as mother, using blue for eyes.
Clothes: Draw and cut out bodice as for mother, but make it longer and looser at waist. Draw and cut out shortened trouser pattern for pants. *Pants.* Make as for father's trousers, either out of broderie anglaise trimming, or of white fabric with lace sewn round trouser bottoms. Put on doll and sew to waist. *Dress.* With right sides facing, sew front bodice to back at sides, shoulders and sleeves. Cut a rectangular piece of fabric approximately 8 in. × $1\frac{1}{4}$ in. or $1\frac{1}{2}$ in. With right sides facing join side seam. Sew line of gathering stitches round top of skirt and pull to match bodice (fig. 124). Sew skirt to bodice. Turn in neck, wrists and skirt hem and sew. Sew two parallel lines of lace to either side of bodice from front to back, and a row of lace horizontally round skirt. Sew ribbon over join and tie in bow at back. Put on doll, and sew up back opening. *Shoes.* Make as for father.

Fig 124

Son

Materials
Body as daughter (i.e. with white legs); light brown 3- or 4-ply wool (yarn); embroidery thread for features; brown or grey cotton fabric; white felt for collar and cuffs; tiny coloured beads for buttons; brown, grey or black felt for shoes.

To make
Body: Make basic doll as for daughter.
Hair: Using light brown wool, sew loops all over head.
Features: Embroider as for mother.
Clothes: Draw and cut out jacket as for mother's bodice, but with front opening and allowing a small overlap. Draw and cut out shortened trouser pattern. *Trousers.* Make as for Father, but three-quarter length to show white stockings. Put on doll and sew to waist. *Jacket.* With right sides facing and front opening, sew front to back at sides, shoulders and sleeves. Trim and turn right side out. Turn in waist hem and sew. Put on doll, turn in front opening and sew together. Sew on beads to look like buttons. Cut wide circular collar out of white felt (rather like the brim of a hat, see chapter 2) and sew to neck with opening at front. Cut two narrow strips of white felt for cuffs and sew to wrists. *Shoes.* Make as for father.

Housekeeper

Materials
Body as basic doll (page 82); white 3- or 4-ply wool (yarn); embroidery thread for features; light blue or grey striped cotton fabric; 2-in.- and 1-in.-wide lengths of white broderie anglaise or lace trimming; narrow white ribbon; white cotton fabric for mob cap; grey felt for shoes.

To make
Body: Make basic doll as for mother.
Hair: Using white wool, sew long stitches all round from front hairline to centre back above nape of neck. Bring needle out at nape of neck. Wind several loops of wool round your little finger and place at back of head. Sew through centre and over loops all round to form a bun and sew firmly to head (see chapter 2).
Features: Embroider as for mother, with white for eyebrows.
Clothes: Dress. Make exactly as for mother (without lace trimming). The skirt could be slightly longer and then given a tuck at hem as for Mrs Moppety (page 27). *Apron.* Cut a piece of 2-in. broderie anglaise or lace trimming long enough to go round dress. Cut a small section of 1-in. broderie anglaise or lace and sew to top of apron at centre front. Hem cut ends if necessary and sew narrow white ribbon ties at back. Put on doll, stitch apron bib to front of dress, tie ribbons in bow at back. *Cuffs.* Cut lengths of 1-in. broderie anglaise or lace to make wide cuffs and sew to sleeves at underside of arms. *Mob cap.* Cut two circles of white cotton about $2\frac{1}{2}$–3 in. in diameter. Make cap as for Mrs Moppety on page 27 (you can use cotton for gathering instead of shirring elastic), and sew to head so that bun is visible at back. *Shoes.* Make as for father.

Chef

Materials
Body as for basic doll (page 82); black 3- or 4-ply wool (yarn); embroidery thread for features; white cotton fabric; white felt; black felt for shoes and buttons.

To make
Body: Make as for basic doll.
Hair: Using black wool, sew long stitches all round head as for father.
Features: Embroider as for father. Make moustache by sewing through a short length of black wool, gluing or sewing it to the face above mouth, and 'waxing' moustache ends with a little quick drying glue.
Clothes: Trousers. Make as for father, using white cotton. Put on doll and sew to waist. *Jacket.* Make as son's jacket, out of white felt and allowing a bigger overlap at front. Put on doll and sew together at front overlap. Make sure neck, wrists and jacket bottom have neatly cut edges. Cut eight tiny black circles out of felt and glue to front in two rows of four. *Hat.* Make a cylinder out of white felt to fit the top of the doll's head and about $1\frac{1}{2}$ in. high. With right side facing join seam. Trim and turn right side out. Cut a circle in white cotton twice the diameter of the cylinder, sew a line of gathering stitches round the outer edge, pull to gather and sew to inside of top of cylinder (fig. 125). *Shoes.* Make as for father.

Fig 125

Butcher

Materials
Body as for basic doll (page 82); grey 3- or 4-ply wool (yarn); embroidery thread for features; white felt; grey felt or fabric; scrap of blue felt for bow tie; dark blue and white striped cotton and narrow blue ribbon for apron; black felt for shoes; thin buff card or stiff paper and red felt for hat.

To make
Body: Make as for basic doll.
Hair: Using grey wool sew long stitches all round head as for father.
Features: Embroider as for father, using grey wool for eyebrows. Sew small grey wool loops for moustache.

Clothes: Trousers. Using grey felt make as for father. Sew to doll at waist. *Shirt.* Using white felt, make as chef's jacket but without overlap. Put on doll and sew together at front. Cut a wide strip of white felt for collar and glue or sew it to shirt at neck. Cut bow shape out of blue felt and glue or sew to shirt. *Apron.* Cut out a rectangle of dark blue and white striped fabric, chest to knee length and wide enough to go round doll. Cut out squares at two corners for the arms, leaving a bib at front. Turn in and hem raw edges all round. Sew blue ribbon ties to waist at back opening and a halter to top of apron front. Put on doll and tie in bow at back. *Hat.* Use thin buff card, or stiff paper. Measure circumference of doll's head, multiply by 7 and divide by 22—this gives you the approximate diameter of the crown. Follow the method used for the top hat in chapter 2 (page 15), using the diameter measurement for the circular crown piece and the inside circle of the brim, and the circumference measure for the length of the side piece, which should be much shallower than that for the top hat. Cut a narrow strip of red felt and glue it round boater as a hatband. If you wish, you can sew the hat to the head to keep it in place. *Shoes.* Make as for father.

Further suggestions

Most of the characters in this book can be adapted to make miniature dolls. Historical characters, national dolls, guardsmen, policemen, Beefeaters, etc., can be adapted from illustrations and picture postcards.

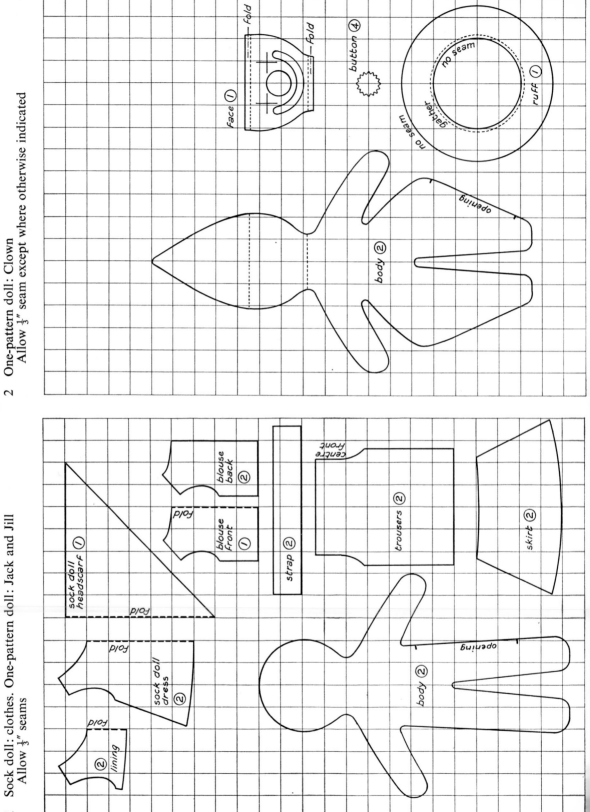

1 Sock doll: clothes. One-pattern doll: Jack and Jill
   Allow $\frac{1}{3}$" seams

2 One-pattern doll: Clown
   Allow $\frac{1}{3}$" seam except where otherwise indicated

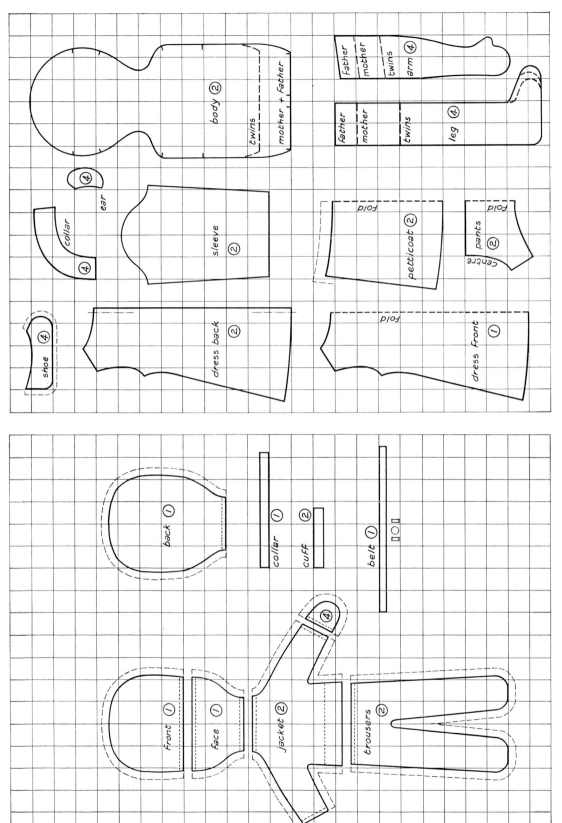

3 One-pattern doll: Guardsman
Allow seam only where indicated

4 Single-hinge doll: basic body; Mother
Allow $\frac{1}{3}$″ seam except where otherwise indicated

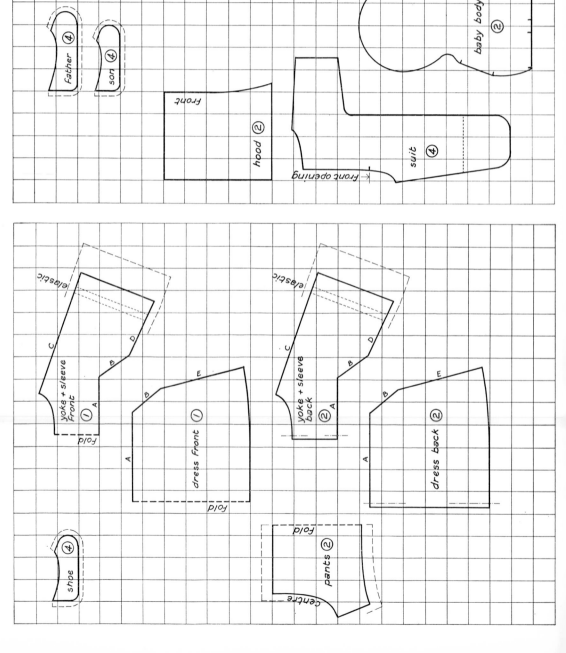

6 Single-hinge doll: Father; Son; Baby
Allow $\frac{1}{3}''$ seam except where otherwise indicated

son: shorts ②

Father: trousers ②

son: shorts centre Fold

pocket ②

waistband ①

arm ④

leg ④

father ④

son ④

hood ②

Front

baby body ②

suit ④

Front opening

5 Single-hinge doll: Daughter
Allow $\frac{1}{3}''$ seam except where otherwise indicated

yoke + sleeve front ① elastic

yoke + sleeve back ② elastic

dress front ①

dress back ②

shoe ④

pants ②

centre Fold

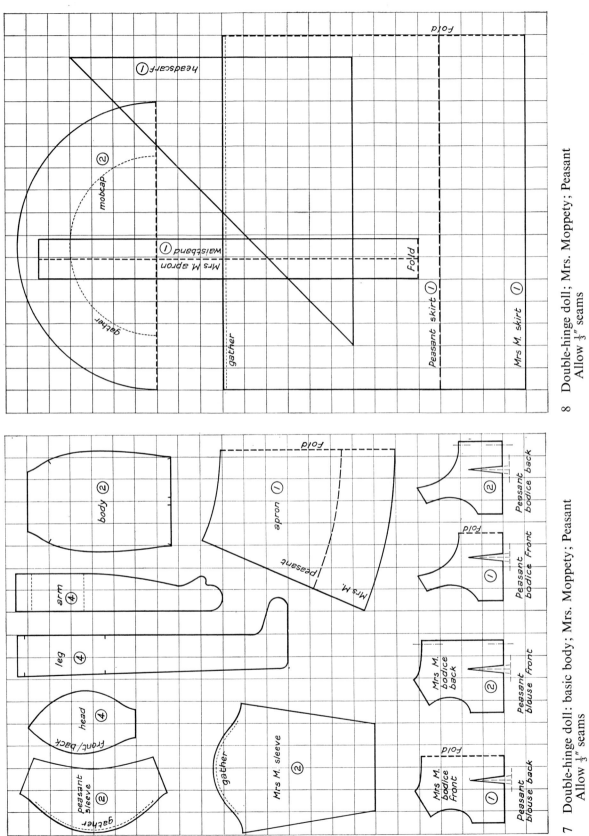

8 Double-hinge doll; Mrs. Moppety; Peasant
Allow $\frac{1}{3}$" seams

7 Double-hinge doll: basic body; Mrs. Moppety; Peasant
Allow $\frac{1}{3}$" seams

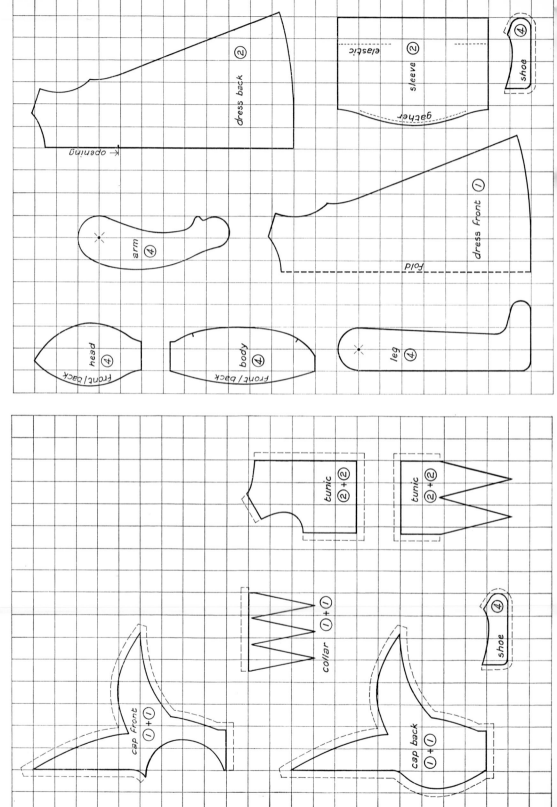

10 Pivot joint doll: basic body; dress
Allow $\frac{1}{3}''$ seam except where otherwise indicated

dress back ②

sleeve ②

elastic

gather

shoe ④

opening →

arm ④

Fold

dress front ①

head ④
Front/back

body ④
Front/back

leg ④

9 Double-hinge doll: Jester
Allow seam only where indicated

tunic ②+②

tunic ②+②

collar ①+①

shoe ④

cap front ①+①

cap back ①+①

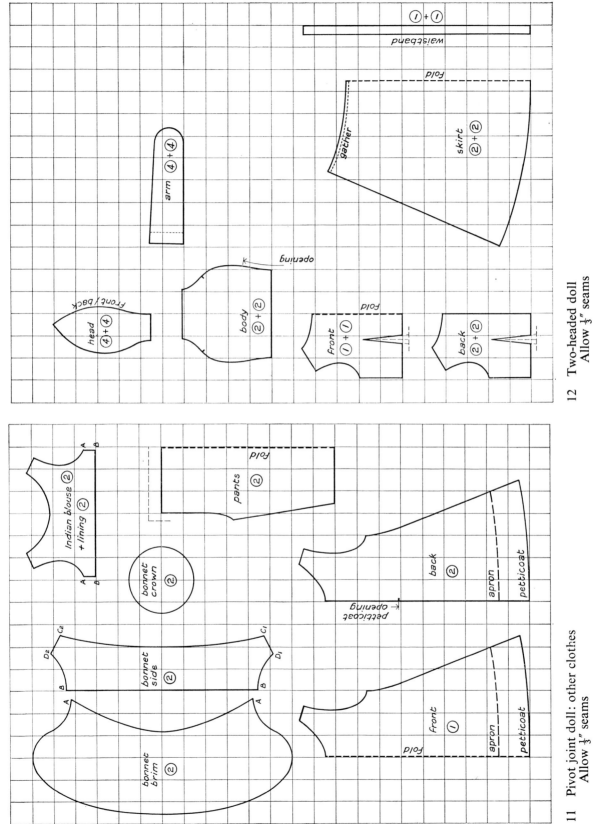

12 Two-headed doll
  Allow ¼″ seams

11 Pivot joint doll: other clothes
  Allow ¼″ seams

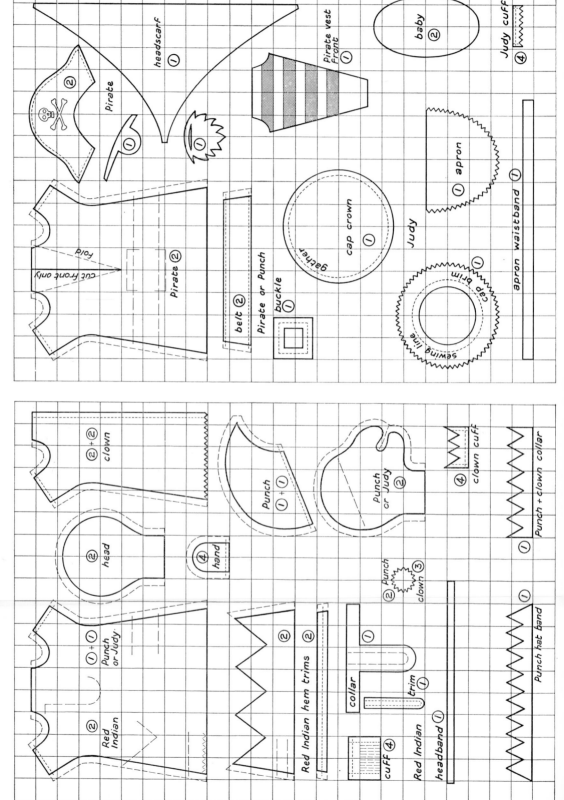

13 Glove puppets: Red Indian; Clown; Punch and Judy
Allow seam only where indicated

14 Glove puppets: Pirate; Punch and Judy; Baby
Allow seam only where indicated

Selected Books

General interest
Dolls and Dollmakers, Mary Hillier; Weidenfeld & Nicolson, London and Putnam, New York, 1968
Dolls of the World, Gwen White; Mills & Boon, London and Branford, New York, 1962
European and American Dolls, Gwen White; Batsford, London, 1966
Dolls, Antonia Fraser; Weidenfeld & Nicolson, London and Putnam, New York, 1963
Dolls Houses, Jean Latham; A. & C. Black, London and Scribner's, New York, 1969

Practical and Reference
Dressing Dolls, Audrey Johnson; G. Bell & Sons, London and Branford, New York, 1969
How to Repair and Dress Old Dolls, Audrey Johnson; G. Bell & Sons, London and Branford, New York, 1967
Making Soft Toys, Gillian Lockwood; Studio Vista, London and Watson-Guptill, New York, 1967
Design Your Own Stuffed Toys, Anne Dyer; G. Bell & Sons, London and Branford, New York, 1969
The Batsford Book of Sewing, Ann Ladbury, London, 1970
Standard Processes in Dressmaking, E. Lucy Towers; University of London Press, 1954
Streamlined Dressmaking, Renée and Julian Robinson; Bodley Head, London and Crown, New York, 1966
Simple Stage Costumes, Sheila Jackson; Studio Vista, London and Watson-Guptill, New York, 1968
Costume Through the Ages, James Laver; Thames & Hudson, London and Simon & Shuster, New York, 1964
Costume in Pictures, Phyllis Cunnington; Studio Vista, London and Dutton, New York, 1964
Fashion through Fashion Plates, Doris Langley Moore; Ward Lock, London and Crown, New York, 1971

UK Suppliers

John Lewis & Co. Ltd,
Oxford Street,
London W.1.
(and branches of the John
Lewis Partnership)

Fabrics, felt, haberdashery, other accessories.

The Needlewoman,
146 Regent Street,
London W.1.

Needlework, embroidery threads, felt, kapok and washable Kaperfill.

Bourne & Hollingsworth Ltd,
Oxford Street,
London W.1.

Haberdashery, wool, etc.

Liberty & Co. Ltd,
Regent Street,
London W.1.

Fabrics.

The Felt and Hessian Shop,
34 Greville Street,
London E.C.1.

Felt (including flooring felt).

F. G. Kettle,
127 High Holborn,
London W.C.1.

Cardboard, paper, cardboard roll (for glove puppets).

branches of H. J. Ryman Ltd

Squared paper and other stationery, glue

Dryad, (Mail Order)
Northgates,
Leicester.

Toymaking tools and accessories, felt, stockinette, calico, cotton flock filling, drawing instruments, needlework, embroidery threads, etc.

Bristol Handicrafts,
20 Park Row,
Bristol 1.

as Dryad, and including rayon filling.

US Suppliers

US readers are advised to go to their local fabric shops, five-and-ten-cent stores, needlework shops, or the notions and fabric sections of department stores for the fabrics, fillings, threads, yarns, needles, and other sewing accessories mentioned in this book. Cardboard, squared (graph) paper, as well as drawing implements and other tools, may be obtained in art supply stores.

Index